cottage
style

Better Homes and Gardens® Books
Des Moines, Iowa

Better Homes and Gardens® Books
An imprint of Meredith® Books

Cottage Style
Editor: Denise L. Caringer
Contributing Editor: Candace Ord Manroe
Art Director: Nancy McGrath Keables
Copy Editors: Jean Ellis, Debra Morris Smith
Proofreader: Kathleen Poole
Electronic Production Coordinator: Paula Forest
Editorial and Design Assistants: Barbara A. Suk, Jennifer Norris, Karen Schirm
Production Director: Douglas M. Johnston
Production Manager: Pam Kvitne
Assistant Prepress Manager: Marjorie J. Schenkelberg

Meredith® Books
Editor in Chief: James D. Blume
Design Director: Matt Strelecki
Managing Editor: Gregory H. Kayko

Director, Sales & Marketing, Retail: Michael A. Peterson
Director, Sales & Marketing, Special Markets: Rita McMullen
Director, Sales & Marketing, Home & Garden Center Channel: Ray Wolf
Director, Operations: Valerie Wiese
Vice President, General Manager: Jamie L. Martin

***Better Homes and Gardens*® Magazine**
Editor in Chief: Jean LemMon
Executive Interior Design Editor: Sandra S. Soria

Meredith Publishing Group
President, Publishing Group: Christopher M. Little
Vice President, Consumer Marketing & Development: Hal Oringer

Meredith Corporation
Chairman and Chief Executive Officer: William T. Kerr
Chairman of the Executive Committee: E.T. Meredith III

All of us at Better Homes and Gardens® Books are dedicated to providing you with the information and ideas you need to enhance your home. We welcome your comments and suggestions about this book. Write to us at: Better Homes and Gardens® Books, Do-It-Yourself Editorial Department, 1716 Locust St., Des Moines, IA 50309–3023.

A Cottage of Your Own

When we bought an old house fifteen years ago, my husband and I saw the chance to make a cherished cottage fantasy materialize—in an unlikely place. Accessible off a second-floor hallway, the attic above the garage was labelled "storage" on the floor plan. But the first time we looked inside and saw its steeply pitched roof and low knee walls, we knew that the "country barn" of our dreams was close at hand. We nailed pine car siding to the ceiling and painted it white, replaced a small window with a glorious new one, and turned skinny collar ties into massive "beams" with wide cedar planks. In no time at all, what had been a dark storage room became our magical getaway—and all we had to do was walk up the stairs to reach it. Whether you live in a delightful cottage—or simply wish you did—this book shows you how to use decorative elements to create the relaxing retreat of your own dreams. What'll it be? A waterfront cottage? A cabin in the woods? A lace-curtained farmhouse? Put your getaway fantasies to work, and you can turn your dreams into reality—right now and wherever you live.

Denise L. Caringer

EDITOR, COTTAGE STYLE

table of contents

COTTAGE STYLE

The away-from-it-all feeling of that lake house or mountain cabin you've always wanted is closer than you think. In fact, your own dreamy retreat may lie within the very room in which you are sitting right now. Although the dictionary defines "cottage" as a usually small vacation home, cottage-style decorating gives you the tools to turn any home into a great getaway. Here, we acquaint you with the elements of some traditional cottage looks. As you turn the pages, put yourself in the pictures. When something—a color, an accessory, a feeling—tugs at your emotions, you'll know it's meant for you.

Finding Your Cottage Colors

Love the romantic look? Here's how you can create a pastel palette for your own painterly cottage style.

■Take your room's "visual temperature." You may want to cool down a sunny, south-facing room with blues and greens, or warm a sunless north-facing one with pinks and peaches. ■ Let colors change your mood. You can energize living and dining spaces with warm pastels but quiet bedrooms with cooler colors. ■Once you've chosen a dominant color, add one or more contrasting pastels, playing warm colors against cool ones for liveliness. ■ Use white trim and furnishings to sharpen the contrast of other hues and to enhance the airy dreaminess. ■Be playful with fabrics that foster the getaway spirit and pull the palette together. For instance, tie or tack contrasting ribbon around ready-made toss pillows (as if wrapping a gift).

RAINBOW'S PROMISE
— beach-house style

The getaway spirit of a sunlit "waterfront cottage" can be yours—wherever you live and whatever your budget—if you start with a mix of pastels that conjure up images of sea and sky. The idea is simple: Roll and brush on a mix of these dreamy tints, from sunset pinks and corals to watery blues, to transform any room into a softly lit romantic retreat. Not only does painted-on style work without a resort location, but it also performs its decorative sleight of hand with or without intrinsically appealing architecture. Start by painting your walls with the palest of pastels to evoke dreaminess, then choose a contrasting and more intense pastel to highlight a handful of key architectural features. Lavish use of cloud-white paint provides the sparkle. The result? An escape from workaday whites into a storybook realm of sea foam and sunsets, no matter the address. The easygoing mix of colors also defines a casual approach to living that relaxes the psyche, reinforcing one of the few necessities of cottage-style decorating—an irreverently lighthearted attitude.

Even a pint-size sleeping nook gains cottage style when its paneled walls are lightened and brightened with pink paint trimmed in white. To save space in snug spots, mount swing-arm lamps on the wall and let a foot-of-the-bed table or chest replace nightstands. No window? Affix a piece of acrylic mirror to the back of an old window to hang behind the bed.

Pink pastel walls give this room a sunset glow no matter what the hour or the season. For cool refreshment, the French doors are painted Caribbean blue. Here, the printed fabrics unite the pink and blue colors, but a bold mix of cool and warm solid-color fabrics would work, too. Imagine pink pillows piped in blue-green!

RAINBOW'S PROMISE

— wrap up in pastels

Forget pedigree, provenance, and somber palettes, and follow these steps to create your own lighthearted mood.

RELEASE YOUR INHIBITIONS with color. A no-fail, one-color-plus-white scheme is a good place to start—but why stop there? Give your favorite pastel a couple of harmonious friends. A dynamic tricolor scheme of lavender, blush, and mint, for example, will add cheeriness, charm, and even a touch of frivolity to a plain modern-day space.

BE INSPIRED by a favorite fabric, painting, or poster on which to base your color scheme if you're unsure of your own color mix. Take the colors right to the walls, windows, ceilings, and doors.

ADD PAINTED PIECES. Chairs and chests, whether unfinished or from a flea market, lend summery beach-house flavor—all year long—when cloaked in pastels or whites.

Accents of white paint applied on this living room's moldings, baseboards, window trim, and ceiling beams provide transition between the three different pastels painted on the walls and ceilings. All of the pastel hues are of the same intensity (or brightness) and all feature a similar saturation of color, making them compatible within a single space. The lavish use of white on the woodwork and in the furnishings not only serves to connect the space, but it also provides the important contrast that highlights each pastel tint.

COTTAGE CUE. Get some vacation-house feeling going by rolling on a coat of pale pastel paint. Use less intense pastels on the walls, and rely on the brighter, more saturated colors to provide bold accents on furniture or trim.

TOUCHABLE TREASURES

Blue and white pottery brings cottage style to a Victorian vanity that's "dressed" to match in decorative paint. To delight the eye and bring out the child in yourself, mix full-scale pieces with miniatures. (Can you really resist picking up those teeny cups?)

While accessories imbue any decorating style with some character, it's the collection of well-loved objects that actually sets the mood in a cottage-style room by anchoring it in a particular place or time. Depending on your style, these objects of affection can be as romantic as faded photographs, porcelain thimbles, and old lace or as rugged as vintage fishing rods, creels, and lures. All that matters is that they are culled by the same adoring eye and displayed for everyone to enjoy.

COME A LITTLE CLOSER. Because cottage style embraces looks that are happy, humble—and definitely hands-on—avoid overly precious pieces that say, "Keep away." Instead of priceless breakables, rely on objects that invite both a lingering look and a loving touch.

GO SLOW. Touchable treasures offer a bonus that goes beyond decorating; small or richly detailed, cottage collectibles invite a leisurely inspection that relaxes rooms by slowing the pace. After all, the subtle coloration of a favorite shell or the handpainted swirls on an old teacup and saucer *do* require some studying.

Choose cottage collectibles you can live with. Mixed with seashells and ribboned straw hats, vintage textiles from several eras invite plopping down in this bedroom. To create your own cohesive mix, do a little dreaming before you start collecting. Conjure up a vision of the look and feeling you love, then put a name to it. This room might be called " summer romance by the the sea."

Create a cottage corner filled with lots to touch and see. Start with an overstuffed chair, then add vintage textiles, framed prints, carved wooden shelves, and, of course, flowers fresh from the garden or the market.

Making Your Arrangements

How you arrange your treasures is just as important as your collectibles themselves. Follow these tips to success.

■ There is power in numbers, especially when working with small objects. For decorating punch, group related pieces instead of scattering them around the house. Favorite teapots, for instance, serve up focal-point impact when gathered on a shelf. ■ When composing an arrangement, delight your eye by varying the size, scale, and texture of objects. ■ On shelves or tabletops, arrange collections so that the edges of individual objects overlap in a cozy way. ■ Group items that share the same shape or function, such as pitchers, teacups, or old glass milk bottles ■ Use color as a visual link. Mismatched glassware, for instance, becomes a happy family when each piece is the same hue, such as cobalt or cranberry.

FAMILY FARM
—back to basics

Inspired by the pristine glow of painted or whitewashed pickets, porch rails, and poultry sheds, farmhouse-inspired cottage rooms literally pale in comparison to their darker, more ubiquitous country cousins. Yet country fans still find them comfortingly familiar. Pine enjoys a place of honor in both styles, but in the cottage farmhouse, the wood often gets a milky coat of paint for a more feminine, decorative finish. Backgrounds, too, appear clean-scrubbed, as though just freshened with whitewash. Even if your "cottage" is in suburbia, you can set the stage for your own harmonious rendition of farm style.

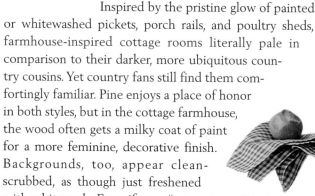

COVER PLAIN WALLS with wood planks or ordinary paneling that's primed, then painted with one or two coats of white.
USE AIRY FABRICS in checks, stripes, or geometric quilt motifs for no-nonsense style.
PRUNE ACCESSORIES way back for nostalgia without fuss. One bold, bucolic object—a sculptural windmill weight or an old watering can overflowing with roadside blooms—can stand in for a whole cottage collection.
UNDERSCORE the simple look with new wood flooring. Install the real thing—oak or pine—or consider surprisingly realistic laminate flooring that mimics natural or stained pine, knots and all.

A small bedroom can acquire a country cottage look when you work from the walls in. Start with wood paneling or with wide planks of wood applied either horizontally or vertically, then brush on the white paint or white stain. For rustic character, prop up artwork on a painted beam hung at chair-rail height. Whether flea-marketing or shopping for new furnishings, look for simple pieces. With timeworn finishes, this new shutter-style headboard and a bedside chest with bun feet add character without fuss.

Straightforward yet charming, farmhouse design is easy to create—and live with. The recipe? Pare your palette to white plus timeless blue, and leave windows and floors unadorned. Here, shapely chairs, pitchers, and hats play off rough wood walls for rustic romance.

Farmhouse Flavor

Simplicity is what makes farmhouse-inspired schemes so easy on the psyche. Use these ideas to give backroads serenity to your own rooms.

■Cut the "background noise." Relax your walls with oh-so-simple white paint, then reduce furniture clutter to a few necessary and well-loved pieces. ■ Limit patterns. Geometric quilt designs and gingham-inspired checks add charm while projecting straightforward farm-style sensibilities. ■Put an "apron" on your chairs. Tie-on slipcovers soften and add a casual look to new dining chairs. ■Bare your panes. Untreated windows enhance the farmhouse feeling. Need privacy? Opt for simple white curtains or shutters. ■Let accessories carry out the mood. A few well-chosen barn or farmhouse posters, old pitchers, quilts, and straw hats surround modern-day lamps and electronics with rural romance.

FAMILY FARM
—Gothic romance

Even in farm country, cottage style has more than one face. With richly detailed wooden trim, a "Carpenter Gothic" home like this may be located just down the road from simpler farmhouses. To adapt the look:

INSTALL A PLATE RAIL with scalloped edging above painted paneled walls. Then gather and display pretty but practical accessories, such as these creamware pitchers and plates.

Cottage country style prefers functional furnishings, such as punched-tin pie safes, over finer carved highboys or cupboards. A touch of ivy in a pot adds a similar old-fashioned feeling. In addition to giving bold architectural presence to this room, the new plate rail with its decorative edging earns its keep as a useful place for displaying prized pitchers and plates. To put your own room together, copy the Victorians' penchant for tables and other surfaces on which to prop up gatherings of framed family photos—and don't forget the doilies!

COMBINE OLD AND NEW. Modern-day comforts gain vintage, down-home style when you build a scheme around new seating pieces inspired by the past. Consider sofas with bun feet and rolled arms and leggy turned-wood chairs, all clad in a congenial mix of pretty florals, stripes, and classic gingham checks. For a feminine touch, let at least one seating piece wear a dainty gathered skirt.

RAISE YOUR SIGHTS by replacing a low coffee table with a taller tea table, plain or skirted, to suggest gracious gatherings of the past.

LIGHTEN THE PALETTE with creamy colors. Starchy-white curtains and garden-fresh wallpaper with a white or pastel background give a room like this a Sunday-best touch without losing its rural airs.

COTTAGE CUE. No Victorian Gothic window? Get the feeling with reproduction furnishings and gingerbread detailing. To take the look to the limit, install a new stove—woodburning or gas—that mimics the charming cast-iron designs of a century ago.

Mixing Fabrics

If your dreams of a cottage getaway take you to the English countryside, then trips to the fabric store and upholsterer are a must. A homey layering of fabrics adds color and pattern and imparts a sense of age.

■Forget matching sofas and chairs and, instead, mix styles, woods, and fabrics to recreate the snug appeal of old family homes in which several generations of furnishings peacefully coexist. ■For mixing without clashing, keep the color family consistent. ■Start with at least one fabric that contains all the hues in your desired palette, and let other fabrics take their color cues from it. ■Vary the scale of patterns, using large, medium, and small prints. ■Florals and vines are an obvious starting point for pattern, but if your room begins to look overgrown, add some visual relief. Just remember your geometry and bring in a chair or pillows covered in stripes or checks.

ENGLISH AMBIENCE

— rooms in bloom

Given England's often gray days, it's no surprise that its cottage style evokes summer romance, all year-round. Pattern is imperative to the English cottage, and cheery florals are the mainstay motif. The fabrics of choice? Chintzes, those cottons with a crisp, polished finish. To create rooms to lift your own spirits, "plant" a variety of floral fabrics to lead the eye around the room in delightful discovery. Start with a blooming sofa, pile on heaps of decorative throw pillows, then gather flowers in generous cascades at the windows. Ample soft seating is another essential; after all, the English virtually invented comfort when they introduced the wing chair. Plan on at least one upholstered piece— perhaps a wing chair or fat roll-arm sofa—to snuggle into when your own skies are gray.

Think cozy. A fabric screen along with a natural-wicker chair dressed in flowered chintz give English-cottage warmth to a potentially cold corner. A wicker table and an armful of flowers— fresh from the grocery store if necessary— evoke dreams of a summer garden, while a soft throw invites a long winter's nap.

England's classic cottage style brings the look of the coveted English garden indoors for year-round enjoyment. The overstuffed chintz-covered sofa is dressed in flowery splendor, but checks and stripes keep the flowers from overpowering. The wood floor is trellised with an ivy pattern painted on as tile-size diagonal checks. For a feminine finish at the windows, lacy sheer panels drop from a ruffled valance.

ENGLISH AMBIENCE

—accents on style

Unlike other European cottage styles, which are mainly peasant at root, English cottage style is aristocratic—a result of the landed gentry scaling down after a change in circumstance. That blend of the classic with the comfortable, the imposing with the inviting is still seen today in a style that's a snap to recreate.

USE LARGE-SCALE PIECES to add grand comfort and time-honored style. Overstuffed upholstery with rolled arms or camelback styling and lofty armoires with architectural details, such as pilasters and raised-panel doors, bring venerable style to American homes regardless of their architectural pedigree. Large furnishings even add a bit of grandeur to ordinary spaces; use a tall bookcase, for instance, to visually "raise" a low ceiling.

STRUT YOUR STUFF. A bit of clutter will give heart and soul to your English cottage room. Plates and pottery, figurines and photos all reflect the style's happy embrace of possessions as a link to one's own beloved past.

A faded look of age relaxes English cottage settings. Here, footprints from the past add character to a time-worn tapestry stool while making it clear that this is not a "feet-off" piece. Atop the simple painted bench, a classic Staffordshire dog stands guard beside leather-bound books that proudly show the hands of time. A red and yellow scheme unifies the mismatched patterns of the fabrics and Oriental rug.

English Country Furnishing Tips

English is the dressiest of cottage styles, but it needn't be costly to achieve.

■ If a hand-me-down sofa or chair is structurally sound, revive it with a sprightly floral chintz slipcover. ■ Recycle odd side tables from family or early marriage as display spots for candlesticks, books, or Staffordshire. ■ Forget matched suites of furnishings. Instead, mix wood types and finishes—light, dark, and painted—for a cozily "evolved" look. ■ Let a shelf or a tabletop host a heartwarming "family reunion" of photos displayed in new or flea-market frames with easel backs. Vary the frames' shapes and sizes. Tip: Have old family photos copied, then store the precious originals away from damaging light. ■ Use a remnant of antique fabric to cover pillows or to act as a table runners or a dresser scarf. Save costly yardage for flat window valances or shades.

CAMP-OUT
—mountain's majesty

Soft woolly blankets wearing a lodge palette of berry red and forest green are draped over chairs to instantly create a camp-style cottage look. Rough natural textures—wicker, twig, and knotty pine—enhance the idea of the outdoors brought in. Stacks of out-of-date magazines, old black-and-white photographs, and a pot of cut greens form the finishing touches that can transform your own living room into a cabin-style getaway.

Piles of decorative pillows to promote comfort are a common feature of different cottage styles. In the camp-out cottage, whimsical Indian-portrait patterns cover pillows for a frontier flavor appropriate for the rugged style.

A cozy retreat in the woods is worlds apart from a breezy beach house, yet this rustic camp style reaches out to just as many hearts as its seaside counterpart. After all, the beauty of cottage design is that it offers a getaway mood for nearly everyone. What's *your* pleasure? If your idea of getting away from it all means snuggling under vintage Beacon blankets amid a pine-forest palette and the rough-edged textures of nature, then mountain-flavored cottage camp may be the decorating style for you. This cottage look, patterned after the large hunting lodges or the Adirondacks' "great camps" from the turn of the century, takes the best of those decorative worlds, then condenses it down to cottage size. Even a small, rough-hewn twig table can convey the great outdoors without taking up a great amount of indoor space, and rugged plaid or blanket-inspired fabrics can turn a modern-day sofa into your own camp-style escape pad.

Chinked pine-log walls make great camp backdrops, but there are other options short of architecture. Use freestanding knotty-pine furnishings—especially in the form of tall bookcases or cupboards—or log-patterned wallpaper to set your own rustic mountain scene.

COTTAGE CUE. Change with the seasons. To usher in winter weather in warm camp style, cover chairs with woolly throws or blankets. Come summer, these instant slipcovers whisk back into the closet where they remain until the cool season rolls around again.

CAMP-OUT
—western roundup

Once you create a cabinlike backdrop with wall treatments or architectural furnishings that repeat the woody textures and colors of the forest, call on fabrics to give your home mountain lodge warmth. Remember: the heavier the weight and the more natural the texture, the better. Here are more tips:

SNUGGLE IN with woolens and other densely woven fabrics in Western-inspired plaids, cowboy-style bandanna prints, and woodsy pine-tree patterns.

TURN UP THE HEAT with fiery reds and earth tones that are just right for cocooning. Be aware, though, that all those warm tones can be overpowering unless you plan some relief in the form of crisp white and a few hints of cooling blue or green in accessories.

LOOK OUTSIDE for new or worn sporting goods, such as hunting and fishing gear, horse tack, and snowshoes, to carry your vision of the outdoors in.

This camp-style setting pays homage to the Old West with its horse-print pillows, bandanna curtains, primitive twig furnishings, and sturdy log walls. A witty accent, the rooster lamp shines a little modern-day light on the subject. To adapt the look, snug a twig table or desk beneath a window, and hang curtains from a tree-branch rod. A wooden ladder, simply propped against the wall, can display collectible blankets, quilts, or fabrics.

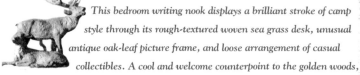

This bedroom writing nook displays a brilliant stroke of camp style through its rough-textured woven sea grass desk, unusual antique oak-leaf picture frame, and loose arrangement of casual collectibles. A cool and welcome counterpoint to the golden woods, piney greens come indoors on the green lamp and heavy cotton curtains.

Give Yourself a Western View

Yes, you can enjoy the rugged, casual style of the West, even if your own "ranch" is in town.

■To create your own rustic "window," hang barn sash on the wall. Salvage old windows, or buy new barn sash at a home center. Hang it as is, or add mirror to reflect your rustic style. ■Use a fallen tree limb or a sturdy twig as a rustic curtain rod. Fabrics cannot slide easily on rough woods, so shop for tab or tie-on side curtains supplemented with shades or blinds for privacy. ■Tie on bandannas for a valance over plain curtains or blinds. ■Hang plaid blankets at the windows for an Old West outlook. Drape them over rods or clip them on with clothespins. ■Corral curtains with tiebacks of rope or even western belts. ■Kick up a little dirt—and a little fun— by using old cowboy boots as planters. ■Display an old saddle or other equestrian gear to echo your room's new-found western "twang."

A LITTLE ROMANCE

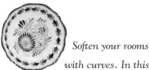

Soften your rooms with curves. In this cottage dining room, scalloped iron chairs and an iron bench with a rounded back pay their respects to romance. Soft lace curtain panels crowned with a swagged and tied valance set the stage for more nostalgic lacework on throw pillows and the table. Flanking the window, gracefully arched shelves display an array of anything but straight-lined objects.

The rough edges of the world outside your door soften and fade when you come home to romance. Instead of evoking some other place or time, this relaxing version of cottage style aims for the most universal target of all: the heart. Fortunately, romance is easy to master, at least when it comes to decorating. Just start with a pure white palette as a canvas for a few shapely details. **BILLOWING, SWAGGING, AND PUDDLING** to the floor, sheer fabric or lace panels bring out the softer side of you and your home. In fact, flowing, lightweight fabrics top the list of romantic essentials. As gossamer as angels' wings, filmy fabrics can skirt tables, beds, and bathroom sinks. But their most dramatic use is at the windows when you choose curtains and valances that include generous gathers. **ROUNDED, SCROLLED, OR LOOPED** shapes found in graceful carvings on wood furniture pieces or in the fanciful designs of metal beds and chairs heighten any room's romantic feelings.

Think of wedding dresses and christening gowns, and you'll know why a pure white-on-white scheme touches the heart. Shapely touches—here in the form of a curlicued iron bed and a puffy comforter—add interest to an all-white room.

AT HOME IN PROVENCE

Maps may argue, but somewhere between light-and-breezy and dark-and-rustic lies the South of France. Its classic country rooms offer yet another interpretation of cottage style—one that blends light and dark, pretty and primitive. No wonder it appeals to decorating moderates who seek tradition—but with a gutsy twist.

USE RICH COLORS. Take your cues from the sun-drenched Provençal landscape, and consider a palette as rich and intense as a Van Gogh painting. Let mustards, terra-cottas, lavenders, and poppy reds extracted straight from the earth play against brilliant celestial blue. If you're unsure of your color palette, the region's brightly colored dinnerware and hand-printed cotton fabrics are sure to inspire you. Such patterns project a peasant flavor with their splashy folk-art designs.

CHOOSE ROBUST FURNITURE. Solid, farmhouse stock softened by a few graceful curves creates the signature blend of the refined with the rustic. Mix finishes—light, dark, painted finishes, and distressed—to give your rooms a sense of age.

A country-French farm table and chairs are downsized to cottage proportions. The chairs' handwoven rush seats provide rustic contrast to their curved slats and legs and lightly washed finish. Quimper plates bring color and folk-art charm to the walls.

Do your own thing—with a French accent. Country-French cottage style has a free spirit that encourages mixing what you love. Here, a family painting, an English Spode platter, and a whimsical bronze mandolin player mingle atop a simple pine chest.

Texture is key to Provençal style. Walls finished with plaster and straw set the peasant-style tone in this living room. The drop-leaf table displays folk-art paintwork characteristic of furnishings in rural French cottages. The style also embraces decorative curves, as displayed on the carved wall shelf.

PURE AND SIMPLE

No excuses now. If you think that creating a fantasy cottage is beyond your budget—of time, energy, or money—think again. You can create a home in which simplicity reigns, where order and absence of fuss make a complex world manageable and the decorating process itself a breeze. Rooted firmly in the here and now, such rooms offer simple coziness without trying to capture the feel of an exotic address or an earlier time. No wonder they're so easy to create.

SET AN AIRY BACKDROP. Team breezy, patternfree walls with simple white sheers, shutters, or shades for easygoing style.

MIX WARM WOODS. New and old pine tables, chairs, and storage pieces can show off their woody tones and textures when the background is plain.

ADD A DASH OF PATTERN. Choose new (or cover cast-off) sofas and chairs in all-American stripes or checks. The sharp graphics and contrasting colors will add decorating punch without trendiness and also serve as canvases on which to layer a few bright, cottage-style floral pillows.

For casual style, let a pine table host mismatched chairs, then add a hutch for instant "architecture." A lineup of colorful plates keeps the eye moving.

Get your living room back to basics with plain-vanilla walls and a natural sisal rug. Here, second-hand furniture gets a lift from fresh slipcovers and toss pillows. The easy finishing touches? Nature's bounty, from fresh fruit to flowers, gathered in china and crocks.

A traditional sign of welcome, this red front door also foreshadows the primary-color palette that lies just inside. Old pine furnishings and outdoorsy accents of watering cans and straw hats lend charm without fuss.

GARDEN FRESH

If your idea of relaxation is an afternoon in the garden, then why not enjoy your favorite garden colors, motifs, and accessories indoors, too? Although all cottages share a knack for dissolving the boundaries between indoors and out, some cottage rooms actually feel as if they are a part of the outdoors thanks to colors, patterns, and accents that make them anything but a subtle imitation of the garden itself. For inspiration, look outside: How does *your* garden grow? You'll always be comfortable if your rooms reflect the materials that you work into your exterior landscape. **MIX LEAFY GREENS** and the bright hues of your own favorite, freshly clipped flowers. Use paint to lavish the color on the wall, or simply introduce it through fabric patterns that include florals, vines, leaves, fruits, or even vegetables. **BLEND TEXTURES** inspired by nature. Wheatlike sisal area rugs and furnishings of wicker, rattan, or twigs play beautifully against soft cotton and smooth painted finishes. **BRING THE GARDEN IN** with birdhouses, garden statuary, and trellis screens. Shop, too, for indoor fountains that can soothe your soul with the sounds of running water all year long.

Instead of rough textures, use soft textiles to create a dreamy cottage-style bedroom that blooms with garden freshness. This splashy floral comforter joins with delicate pillows in floral motifs, while a small bedside area rug puts a colorful field of flowers underfoot. Even the pillowcases are edged in reminders of the garden. White furnishings recall the outdoor charm of freshly painted picket fences.

Turn a corner into an instant indoor garden. The transformation can begin with a bamboo or latticework screen and a birdhouse or two. Clad in soft, floral cotton, a skirted armchair and matching sofa contrast nicely with the natural textures of bamboo and woven wood baskets.

A VINTAGE FABRIC

Nearly any room can be energized with a few vintage textiles used here or there. But when they're allowed to have free rein, with entire collections decorating a home, such fanciful fabrics can stamp an especially exuberant brand of cottage style on any interior space.

Especially suited to collectors who are willing to go out of their way to gather such remnants of the past, this style also is made to order for fans of the 1940s—the decade providing the most prolific and colorful patterned fabrics that are still available and in good shape today. Here's how to get your rooms in the mood.

DECIDE ON THE FEELING you want to create. Obviously, faded florals from the early 1900s will impart a decidedly different look than the bright fruit and vegetable prints of the 1940s and 1950s. Once you pick a mood, whether romantic or bright and funky, stick to it, using color to link your mismatched finds.

PUT FABRICS TO WORK. Cover tabletops with of-the-era cloths, and use decades-old curtains at the windows. (To avoid cutting and sewing precious fabric remnants, simply clip them to cafe rings and hang as instant valances or half-curtains.) Do the unexpected, too, using old dish towels to make curtains and toss pillows, and framing decades-old floral hankies as art.

Bright and beautiful, vivid tablecloths, napkins, and dish towels from the recent past add a spot of cheer to a kitchen eating spot. To create a high-energy scheme, contrast complementary cool and warm colors. Here, red plays off green.

An old quilt or quilt remnant brings a homey look to a dining room when put into service as a tablecloth. To protect the textile, use it for colorful display (versus dining), or top it with a round of clear glass.

A bedroom brings the past up to date with a mix of new and vintage fabrics. The double wedding-ring quilt teams with an embroidered sheet and new decorative pillows and bed skirt. Lacy half-curtains soften a city view.

FABRIC FURNITURE COLOR

So you love cottage style but don't know how to begin to put together your own scheme? Relax. By first breaking the style down into clearly defined parts, you can easily build your own look, one element at a time. This chapter shows how to choose and use fabrics, furniture, and color as tools in creating a cottage look you'll love.

FABRIC
FURNITURE
COLOR

IMAGINE A ROOM WITH WHITE WALLS, BEIGE CARPET, AND PLAIN, PATTERN-FREE FABRICS. NOW, PLAY A GAME OF "mental paper dolls" and visualize covering the seating pieces or bed with fabrics of different colors and patterns. Think about a romantic pastel botanical or floral print. Do you like it? Now, try on a rugged red-and-black buffalo plaid. How does it feel? Or consider crisp blue-and-white cabana stripes or snappy checks. Obviously, the same old furniture pieces can assume fresh cottage-style identities when new fabrics enter the picture. But where to begin? In this section, you'll learn how to mix and match fabrics and wallpapers to create just the look you have in mind. As you thumb through these pages, remember to let your heart be your guide. If you find yourself turning back to look at the same photo over and over again, it must be love.

When you find a favorite fabric, use it and use it. Here a happy floral sets the color scheme as it repeats for the café curtains, accent pillows, and French-style armchair. Buy a supporting fabric, here the check, to reinforce the color scheme and add the dimension of another pattern. For the most pleasing look, repeat your dominant pattern at least three times in a cottage setting.

For a no-fail scheme, use two patterns in the same color—here green and white. Pair a floral with a geometric or stripe to keep the look from seeming overly sweet.

Mix simple sheers at the windows with an open geometric fabric for a more tailored look. Light, open background fabrics keep the look airy and summery.

Pile on the Style With Pillows

Love collecting? Think of building another trove of treasures in the form fabrics—old and new—to cover a mix of toss pillows.

■Look in the linen closet. Consider adapting standard pillow cases in cottage-style florals and ticking stripes, as well as bits of pretty but frayed sheets. Old bedspreads—especially when made of coveted chenille—make charming cottage coverings, too. ■Browse flea markets and tag sales, keeping an eye open for clothing with beautiful fabrics just waiting to be salvaged. ■Check the remnant tables at fabric stores for a wealth of low-cost choices. Imagine what you can do with just one yard of fabric! ■Preserve sections of damaged quilts for cottage pillow toppers. ■Use fabric napkins in fresh ways. With finished hems, they make quick pillow covers. Just insert a pillow form or filling and stitch up the edges. ■Mix pillows of different shapes and sizes for impact.

PILLOWS TALK

Fabric is the design tool that can set your cottage style to music, providing visual rhythm and counterpoint through pattern, texture, and color. Because cottage style is one of the most intimate of interior designs, it makes sense to introduce that visual music through small touches—in decorative details, such as pillows. In fact, you can create your own personal compositions by arranging beautifully patterned, intricately trimmed, and variously shaped beauties.

MAKE IT SNAPPY. Adding fabric through throw pillows is a quick way to cozy up a pattern-less room—and build your design confidence if you're shy with color and pattern. Soften sofas and chairs, and don't forget the bed: Piles of pillows in interesting shapes make this most personal retreat even more alluring.

EXPRESS YOURSELF. Fabrics send different cottage messages, so choose your mood: Is it rustic or refined? Seashore or mountain? Then toss on the appropriate patterns, whether splashy florals, cabana stripes, or outdoorsy textures.

Love nostalgia? Don't fight the feeling. Coupled with old wicker, a muted palette with a slightly faded look of age evokes the serenity of the past. Embellishments of puffy ball trim and fuzzy fringe are details that enhance the pillows' handcrafted appeal.

For cozy appeal, cottage pillows travel in packs. Heaped on a sofa, instead of going it alone, they create visual background music that reinforces your own personal cottage style. These pillows sing of their owner's love of contemporary gardens with strong sparkling color—and nary a faded rose in sight. The use of small-, medium-, and large-scale patterns creates pleasing three-part harmony.

In addition to mixing fabrics in pillow groupings, use a variety of prints on a single pillow to increase visual interest and also to serve as transition with other pillows in an arrangement.

AMAZING LACE

At their best, cottage rooms invite you to relax and linger. Layered with irresistible treasures and textures, these settings simply can't be swallowed up in a single glance. Because of that, lace makes an ideal cottage accent. The subtle patterns found in lace require closer inspection to fully appreciate— a trait in total sync with the style's up-close and intimate character. Yet, no matter how intricate its design and workmanship, lace retains an essentially simple look that's consistent with cottage style's emphasis on the real and unpretentious. Lace also suits cottage-style decorating because of its ease and mixabil-ity; in a flash, lace softens a window, tabletop, or bed skirt, adding instant romance without upstaging your room's other furnishings. Where to use lace? Just about anywhere.

FRAME IT. Vintage remnants look pleasant under glass—a creative way not only to pre-serve but also to present heirloom swatches.

THREAD IT onto a tension rod to create an instant curtain. Why not use a narrow panel to soften a fixed sidelight beside a front door?

HANG IT on a rod suspended from the ceiling to add pattern to clear-glass show-er or tub enclosure, thus charming a chilly modern bath.

LAYER IT over the edges of shelves in a kitchen or a bedroom. Hand-stitch lace fragments or crocheted doilies over the tops of ready-made, solid-color toss pillows.

What could be simpler? A panel of sheer, semi-transparent lace softens any room—or view. Because lace doesn't fea-ture a printed-on pattern or a colorful palette, it has the greatest impact when used alone, with no other curtain treatment; other-wise, its subtlety can be overpowered and its charm gone to waste. However, you can have your lace and privacy, too; simply install an unobtrusive roller shade or blind within the win-dow casing behind the lace.

Display heirloom handkerchiefs and small dresser scarves with lacy cutwork as cottage-style art. Sleek frames put the emphasis on the textiles themselves. The treatment also preserves the fragile textiles from too much handling. Here a scallop-edged dinner napkin used as a dresser scarf integrates the framed pieces into their setting.

To show off an intricate lace design, consider stretching a single flat panel across the width of a window, instead of gathering it. The treatment offers a cottage look as well as a quick-and-easy window solution. Here, the contrast between the dark window trim and white lace adds drama, as does this decidedly European-style shortened length.

FLOWER POWER

Perhaps no motif conveys cottage style's distinctive freshness better than florals. But different flowers, color schemes, and materials can create different moods. Here are some tips to help you choose the right florals for the cottage look that you have in mind.

PICK A FLOWER to express your style. Complex designs of mini prints or cabbage roses are old-fashioned at heart. Choose the cleaner lines of abstract florals or simple flowers such as daisies if your cottage dream is rooted in today.

CHOOSE A PALETTE. Pastels and nostalgia make natural companions, because light tints suggest the faded look of the past. Feeling rustic? Try a more saturated, robust scheme of wildflower colors with cool pine-forest accents. Bold brights can bring cottage schemes up to the present.

USE TEXTURES to foster your mood. Shiny glazed chintzes add a touch of formality, while soft matte cottons or nubby fabrics send a more casual message.

CONSIDER CONTRAST between a fabric or wallpaper background and motif. Brights on a white ground can create bold beach-house flavor; faded flowers on beige will take you to the past.

Hand-painted florals and bold stripes create an irresistibly fresh, summerhouse scheme. Adapt the look by mixing airy floral sheets with spirited striped ones; the white background creates the bright feeling. Feeling arty? Combine fabric paints and your own creativity to personalize plain linens. How about striped hems plus stenciled or freehanded fish or flowers? A cutwork cloth and an array of real blooms make easy finishing touches.

A single floral cotton repeated on chair coverings and window valances unifies this room with cottage style. The stylized rose motif is an update on the past for a look of currency in harmony with heritage. Light color saturation ensures that the fabric doesn't overpower the white setting or negate the airy mood. A natural fiber rug and a solid green-painted table anchor the sitting spot.

Play with Patterns

Have fun and turn stripes, checks, and florals loose in your cottage rooms. Just keep these tips in mind to avoid a pattern free-for-all.

■ Select one color palette—then stick with it—to create unity when mixing several prints in a room. ■ Choose one fabric or textile, such as an area rug, that contains all of the colors in your desired palette. Other fabrics can use any of these hues, as long as they don't add colors outside the original color family. ■ When mixing three or more patterns, vary the scale, using one large, one medium, and one small print. For example, mix a wide stripe on a sofa with a small pinstripe at the windows, and a medium-size floral or check on a chair. ■ Provide visual relief. Include some neutrals and solid colors. Contrast a roomful of patterned fabrics with plain painted walls. ■ When in doubt, learn from the mix masters. Check out the collections of beautifully mixed patterns sold at fabric and wallpaper stores.

MIXED BAG

In this family room two floral fabrics coexist beautifully. Not only do the florals share the same blue-and-white palette, but they also vary in scale so they can sit side by side without competing. Geometrics—in this case snappy hot-pink checked pillows—add spice to any room filled with flowery fabrics.

A bold mix of patterns turns this secondhand chair into a witty cottage accent. A red-and-green palette (accented by red cording) links the three disparate fabric prints.

Perhaps the most lovable quality of cottage style is that it simply refuses to take itself too seriously. What that means is that you, too, can relax during the decorating process. Of course, standard guidelines for good design apply. But to get your rooms in just the right cozy mood, go ahead and stretch your own sense of "the rules," especially when it comes to mixing patterns. Cottage design is essentially a happy, naive look, and a bold mix of different patterns can convey that almost childlike sense of play.

Although it appears to be an art, mixing patterns is a craft you can master using the tips on page 46. To build your confidence, start by tossing a striped or checked pillow onto a floral sofa or comforter—or adding a floral pillow to a striped sofa. See? Mixing is no big deal. At its freewheeling best, this spontaneous style welcomes a mix of different motifs—often on a single furniture piece.

RETRO

It's little wonder that the retro fabrics of 1940s and 1950s kitchens have found a beloved niche in cottage design. The high spirits of their bold Fiestaware colors and charming motifs (from cherries to checks) make them a natural choice when you want a room to send a bright wake-up call to your psyche.

FIND AN INSTANT PALETTE. Featuring the same intense colors as Fiestaware, these prints commonly combine an entire spectrum of bold hues on a single fabric. Pick an old tablecloth, and your color scheme is set.

GET A PATTERN MIX, TOO. Many retro fabrics incorporate several different floral and geometric motifs on a light background. Choose one or two old fabrics to set your room's scheme, then fill in the gaps with new fabrics that repeat a color, motif, or feeling.

HAVE FUN putting these fabrics into service. Browse flea markets and garage sales for 1940s dime-store tablecloths, dish towels, or napkins. Then combine your finds at the windows in light-heartedly mismatched valances or on the chairs in the form of fresh cushion covers. Even if the fabrics vary, their frankly fun design themes will provide all of the visual continuity you need.

Forget changing the curtains or re-covering the sofas— this look is achieved simply by plopping down pillows wherever you like. First scour flea markets for great finds, then do a little recycling. If the filling in old pillows is in poor condition but the fabric is intact, reuse the fabric for new pillows. Often, damaged fabric can be cut down for small pillow covers.

Novelty-print pillows from decades past provide quick access to cottage style. Recycling retro fabric remnants as decorative pillows is one of the easiest, fastest ways to create your own unique cottage look.

Whether made of 1940s tablecloths or new yardage that mimics the look of that era, bold and bright fabrics will reenergize your kitchen. Old artificial fruits still retain their decorative function, but this time as clever curtain tiebacks. Echoed by the table's boldly painted edge, new checked seat cushions pick up the colors—and happy spirit—of the curtains.

FABRIC
FURNITURE
COLOR

COTTAGE STYLE IS FORGIVING, FLEXIBLE, AND FUN—THREE TRAITS THAT MEAN RELIEF FOR ANYONE PUZZLED ABOUT PUTTING

Beyond the utilitarian, furniture sets the mood. Here, a Victorian-style screen with vintage photographs speaks of the charm of an English cottage. Versatile pieces, such as the wicker and plain farm-style table, adapt to many different settings. Use accessories, such as the exotic mirror from an overseas adventure, to add your own stamp of personality.

Classic charmers, such as the Windsor bench with its crackled paint finish shown at right, can work in living or dining rooms.

together just the right furniture mix. In cottage settings, furnishings that are new and old— even indoor and outdoor—mingle effortlessly. Hand-me-down tables, chests, and chairs—freshly painted or left as is— breathe fresh life into cottage rooms. Outdoor furnishings easily move indoors, bringing a breezy feeling with them. And cushy upholstered pieces, regardless of age, are always welcomed (and often treated to a cottage facelift with fabrics). Favorite cottage staples—small benches and rocking chairs—contribute their own touches of charm. In this section, you'll see that cottage furniture is all about ease and homey comforts, not fancy labels or price tags. What decorating news could be better than that?

Pair antiques, such as the corner cupboard, with upholstered pieces in lively fabrics. When you buy chairs and sofas in classic shapes, they easily can be refreshed with new fabrics, slipcovers, or even accent pillows as your rooms and your taste evolve.

A BRUSH OF WHIMSY

Painted furnishings make decorating fun, creating rooms rich with imagery that's down-home—and often downright cute, too. Whether your dream is of a farmhouse or a cabin at the lake, painted scenes can put the vision from your mind's eye into full view for everyone to enjoy. The new home, at right, for example, gets a fresh farm-style focal point thanks to the trompe l'oeil rabbit hutch painted on the tall cupboard.

START SHOPPING. Some major furniture manufacturers produce pieces that include rural landscapes and other realistic trompe l'oeil images.

COMMISSION A DESIGN if you have a special image or color scheme in mind. Hire a local artist or an art student to paint your cottage view on secondhand or unfinished furniture

DO IT YOURSELF. Yes, even you can "cottage up" any furniture piece if you work with stencils. Much easier to execute than free-handed artwork, stenciling is a favorite approach to painting cottage furniture, especially for those who can't draw a straight line. If you can trace, you can stencil, dabbing on a trail of ivy, a field of flowers, or crisp geometrics taken from classic quilts or checkerboards. Consider, too, accenting cabinet doors or a floor screen with new wall covering and border designs that replicate scenes from the past.

Limit yourself to one major scenic furniture piece per room. Here, a rabbit hutch complete with a bevy of bunnies was custom-painted on the cupboard's doors. The amusing trompe l'oeil scene extends onto the backs of the cabinet doors. To blaze a fresh and fun trail to personal style, the owner mixed the decidedly romantic rabbits with rustic western gear.

This chest's old-fashioned styling and hand-painted panels on front cabinet doors contribute to its English cottage flavor. Look for custom-painted pieces, as well as those produced by major furniture manufacturers.

With its graceful turned legs and delicate proportions, this desk is a perfect canvas for some decorative stenciled ivy trailing over white paint.

Defining Comfort

Not all upholstered furniture is created equal. Use these terms as you shop.

■Rely on "eight-way hand-tied coil-spring construction." It ensures that the best materials and method are used to make an upholstered piece that will comfort you for years. It means that coil springs are held in place across the top by eight hand-tied knots of high-quality webbing, such as imported hemp or Italian jute. ■For cushion fillers, the term to know is HR: high-resilience foam. It holds its shape the best and provides the longest wear. Down is luxuriously soft, but it needs frequent fluffing to maintain its shape. Some cushions blend the two—a foam core wrapped in down. ■Choose kiln-dried hardwood frames for durable seating pieces.

This place promises a soft spot for head, back, and feet with a roll-arm chair, plumped with pillows, and an obliging ottoman nearby.

THE STUFF OF COMFORT

This cottage living room doesn't go wild with fussy backgrounds or accessories. Instead, its comfortable seating (in an easy mix of stripes and florals) delivers the come-hither message—and makes the look especially simple to adapt. Amply proportioned and accented by lace, throws, and downy pillows, the upholstered pieces speak of timeless ease. The sofa's loose-cushioned back and seats ensure soft support.

Mention cottage comfort, and images of sink-down seating, cloud-soft fabrics, and cushy pillows come to mind. Plan for at least one feel-good seating unit—a piece that's just right for settling back, putting your feet up, napping, cuddling with Fido, or simply contemplating the universe. An accommodating sofa, lounge chair or chaise will do. The other essential? An ottoman or even a sturdy coffee table you can prop your feet on after a tough day.

This kind of comfort translates into overstuffed upholstery—timeless traditional shapes with generous proportions and welcoming arms. Look for wide (and often rolled) chair and sofa arms, and consider backs that are loose-cushioned, not tight (fixed in place). Before you buy, plop down and lie back. If your reaction is, "Ah-h-h-h-h," the piece probably is right for you.

ROCK-A-BYE

Do you know the "Three R's" of making a great cottage-style getaway? Rock. Roll. Relax. How can you remain ruffled when a rocking chair's gentle motion leaves you no option but to slow down? The pace may be languid, but it's amazing how far you can go, without going anywhere at all, when you settle back and enjoy the action. With their to-and-fro motion, rocking chairs lift your mind and heart, taking take them to faraway places.

ROCK ON. Happily, you can make your own great escape in just a sliver of floor space—and in any room you want to devote to the simple, homey pleasures of life in the slow lane. Front porches and bedrooms are obvious choices, but don't overlook any neglected corner, even in a dining room. Some cottage designs even enlist the rocking chair at tableside—not the most practical of seats for dining, but certainly one of the best seats in the house for pushing back from the table and visiting with family once the meal is finished.

PICK YOUR STYLE. Cottage rocker styles abound. You may lean toward rustic or wicker rockers that are equally at peace indoors or out or the straight-lined beauty of Craftsman-inspired wood-slat rockers. Don't overlook upholstered rocking chairs if you lean toward a slightly dressier, English-country approach to cottage comfort.

A wood rocking chair with a simple slatted back and seat conveys unpretentious farmhouse cottage style. The only ornamentation is a Gothic-style finial typical of the late 1800s. For summer, the slats go bare, since the curved seat offers plenty of comfort. But when winter arrives, squashy, tie-on seat and back cushions and a soft throw can lend welcome warmth, both to the body and to the eye.

"Age" new wicker. Brush on barn-red paint; sand some off while still tacky. Let dry. Repeat process with light green paint. Some areas should show raw wicker, others a hint of red.

Crafting twig furniture has become a favorite American pastime—good news for fans of rustic cottage style, who can now find an array of twig rocking chairs to use both indoors and out.

One of the most inviting arrangements of all gathers rocking chairs in
a friendly circle. For the front porch, this is a welcome that sets the
tone for the entire house. Here, the wicker rockers are matched for simple
harmony and to avoid upstaging the architectural details of the house itself.

LIGHTHEARTED WICKER

Wicker brings an outdoor palette inside your home. But dressed in blue-and-white patterned fabrics that blend with the rest of your decor, there's no mistaking its indoor function. Covered buttons and fabric tabs secure this soft cushion seat.

Nothing is better than wicker for stirring nostalgia. Flip through design magazines of the 1920s and 1930s, and you'll find wicker holding its own. But its appeal is about more than yearning for another era. For many, wicker can tug at the emotions to soothe in another way: there's comfort in knowing that the same style of furniture that surrounds you today also may have been enjoyed by your grandmother—and hers. **INSIST ON EASE.** It's no wonder that wicker turns up in so many heartwarming cottage rooms today. Beyond nostalgia, wicker sums up cottage style's easygoing nature. Wicker requires minimal maintenance, and it's just as at home on the front porch as in the living room. Although natural wicker cannot be left out in the weather, synthetic all-weather wicker can spend a summer outside without deteriorating. **USE WICKER ANYWHERE.** Besides its breezy style, wicker, no matter how it's finished, mixes with virtually any furnishings—a real plus in cottage rooms that get much of their snug look from layering. Not only does wicker bring the textures of the outdoors inside, but it also can echo nature's palette. Cloud white is a classic choice, but don't overlook natural wicker with its woody color and texture—or painted wicker in any color from sunrise fuchsia to leafy green.

Start with a new chair from the import store, then add your own creative touches. A little fringe, tassels, and a hot-glue gun are all it took to embellish this newly made lady's chair. Consider ornamenting your own wicker with braid or fringe to stir up a little romance. The chair is equally at home in the bedroom or the living room.

White wicker is the common denominator that brings this window grouping of table, lamp, and chair together in restful harmony. Three birdhouses in graduated sizes link this tablescape with the view outside.

ON THE BENCH

Once upon a time, the primitive bench knew its place—just about anywhere, as long as it stopped at the doorstep, never daring to venture inside. Times have changed, especially as cottage style has entered the mainstream and thrown dated notions of design propriety out the window. The plain board bench is showing up in the most surprising places—even in the bedroom or bath.

PUT A BENCH TO WORK. No longer relegated to the garage or garden, the humble bench has become a coveted fixture in cottage furnishings, offering charming style and unlimited versatility at the same time. Use it to hold almost anything, from favorite, just-for-looks collectibles to utilitarian household wares. Because of its low stature, the bench can sidle up to or tuck under leggy tables and chests, serving as a space-efficient repository for books and magazines. A bench also makes a great stand-in for "real" furnishings— as a character-laden coffee table, a bedside nightstand, or a footstool.

SEEK AND FIND. Look for weathered painted benches at antiques shops and flea markets or new unfinished pieces that await your creative finishing touch.

The low, horizontal space beneath a long window becomes an indoor garden spot—thanks to a footstool-size bench that bridges the gap between the floor and sill.

A new crackled green finish on this especially low bench provides a rough-textured counterpoint to the bathroom's slick tile and porcelain. The bench also serves a practical function as a handy shelf for soft towels and toiletries.

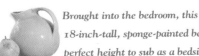
Brought into the bedroom, this 18-inch-tall, sponge-painted bench is the perfect height to sub as a bedside table. There's enough room beneath it for sliding in vintage suitcases or wicker boxes for extra storage.

Let the Sun Shine In

Bringing the outdoors in is as easy as opening up to the idea of using outdoor furnishings in interior spaces. Here's how.

■Before rushing out to your nearest outdoor furniture retailer, first stroll through your own backyard. Chances are, you already own some appropriate pieces for recycling indoors. A fresh coat of paint, skewed to the indoor palette, can reveal untapped potential. ■A wooden picnic table makes every meal festive in its new indoor digs. Consider an old wooden picnic table—redwood-stained or freshly painted—or a new natural pine one from the home center. ■Gliders and porch swings permit wiling away the hours indoors, just as readily as they do outside. ■Analyze old birdbaths and fountains as potential indoor table bases. ■Include outdoor accessories such as birdhouses.

Kick back with Adirondack chairs, weathered signs, and watering cans. The glass tabletop offers sleek and airy contrast.

OUTDOORS IN

Sure, fabrics in sprightly garden colors and motifs can bring the outdoors in. But if you're in love with your garden (or simply have a thing for summer), look for some outdoor furnishings, too, that can give your rooms just the right open-air ambience.

Fresh from performances on the patio or at the local flea market, aged outdoor tables, chairs, benches, and accessories ensure that the livin' is easy in any room in which they're placed. Whether of sturdy wood or weathered metal, they instantly relax interior spaces—and also add vitality simply by carrying the element of surprise. The only rule: Don't limit outdoor furnishings to the sunroom. They delight even more in less expected places. Why not bring the fun of al fresco dining indoors with an outdoor table and chairs? Who says an Adirondack chair can't "live" in the living room?

This garden charm comes from the simplest details: outdoor furnishings, including an old slat-back, slat-seat, iron-frame bench (hardly wider than a chair), an ice-cream-style iron-leg table, and a host of outdoor garden planters.

THE ROMANTICS

Like people, some furnishings are simply more romantic than others. When your goal is to decorate on the romantic side of cottage style, look for furniture with graceful proportions, curved forms, and decorative detailing. These shapely or well-trimmed furnishings abound, even in new furniture collections. Instead of choosing a straight-lined pencil-post bed, for example, look to a canopy bed of curlicued iron. It offers the same reed-thin shape and tall post heights but in romantic form. Then, top it with sheers or mosquito netting allowed to loop, fold, and fall to its own rhythms. For tables and chairs, choose turned legs over straight ones. And don't overlook the romantic possibilities of upholstered seating pieces. You can even give an aging sofa a little love—in all the right places—by adding some frilly pillows or a new slipcover with a daintily gathered skirt.

Romance materializes in the form of a sleigh bed with graceful, curved lines. Although this bed is antique, newly manufactured sleigh beds are not hard to find. Romance also means fabrics and bed linens that are suitably soft, both to the hand and the eye. In this room, a simple portiere hangs at one side, offering a hint of softness and pattern without consuming too much space. This cotton duvet cover with its lavender floral pattern also speaks of romance.

Soften your rooms with inherently romantic furniture pieces that include shaped forms to help your rooms break out of the rigid box. Such curvilinear pieces needn't seem frail or feminine. This antique bed offers the best of both worlds with venerable styling that's solid and stately. It combines visual weight and physical mass with delicacy of shape.

FABRIC
FURNITURE
COLOR

NOTHING AFFECTS HOW A ROOM FEELS MORE THAN ITS COLOR PALETTE. FORTUNATELY, COTTAGE STYLE

Painted furniture can bring a dash of mellow color to any room. Here, the painted pieces work with the neutral background to set the stage for an ever-changing array of colors brought in with dinnerware, accessories, and flowers.

offers an unlimited range of choices. Lights and brights, warms and cools, happy mixes, and serene monochromatics create different but equally beautiful schemes. Pale pastels and whites are conducive to a romantic mood, high-voltage primary colors and vivid multicolor palettes are irrepressibly cheerful, and earthy colors bring nature indoors. With cottage style's emphasis on the heartfelt and homey, the choice depends entirely on your own personal preferences. So, start with your favorite color, then use this section to find just the right companions for it—colors that will create just the mood you want.

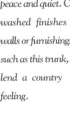

Cool colors, including restful shades of blue and green, create serenity in any room where you want a little peace and quiet. Colorwashed finishes on walls or furnishings, such as this trunk, lend a country feeling.

Busy patterns can get in the way of a pure-and-simple farmhouse scheme. If that's your style, consider warming a room simply with a touch of bright paint.

A PURE PALETTE

It's difficult not to be inspired by rooms done the white way. Not only is white the color of all things pure and pretty—freshly fallen snow, new cream, old lace, and, of course, wedding gowns—but it also speaks of simple serenity. Devoid of jarring color or pattern, a room dominated by soft white makes it easy to relax and let your mind wander.

All it takes is a little white in curtains and wicker to give romance to your rooms. To create the inviting window seat, slide a chaise or sleigh bed beneath the window, then pile on the cushions and throws.

START WITH WHITE on the backgrounds to create your own peaceful place. White walls and ceilings provide a pristine stage on which cottage furnishings can play. Appearing on softer textiles, such as lace and sheers, and on lighter furnishings, such as wicker, other white touches foster the pure look.

KEEP IT SIMPLE by choosing major furnishings that are relatively patternfree. Warm woods and just a smattering of floral fabrics can add warmth without overpowering the dominant whites.

ADD TEXTURES for vital warmth. In addition to wicker or wood, add textured fabrics, such as chenille or matelassé.

Primitive or dark wood cottage furnishings stand out in silhouette fashion when used in a color palette that's dominated by white. White walls, bedding, and furniture upholstery give this bedroom its clean and simple charm. The only other hues—pale pastels on the area rug—are so subtle they don't detract from white's purifying presence.

Teamed with quilts and florals, lots of white (on wood-clad walls, in curtains, wicker, lace, rag rug, and matelassé bedspread) creates farmhouse romance.

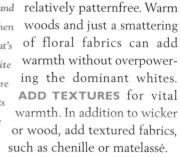

Analogous Color Schemes

Whether soft and subtle or bright and bold, an analogous color scheme of three or more neighboring hues makes color mixing easy.

■Consult the color wheel, and use three or more hues that are adjacent to one another on it. For the highest-energy scheme, include both warm and cool colors. ■Pick colors of the same intensity so each hue carries equal weight. Intensity refers to how bright or dull the color is. ■Feeling a bit timid? Pull your room together easily by using the same color on all the backgrounds and the other two to three colors as accents in upholstery and accessories. ■Choose your mood. For high energy (say, in a kitchen), let warm colors dominate. To relax a bedroom, emphasize cool hues. ■Reshape space. Cool colors visually retreat while warm colors advance. That's why walls painted a warm color seem to wrap you like a hug.

SPECIAL BLENDS

Color trends come and go, but the basics—and your own good gut instincts—never change. Chances are that if you love blue today, you'll still love it twenty years from now. And why not? Start with that favorite color, then look to the color wheel to create these especially easy schemes. If you lean toward subtle color, relax; any colors on the wheel can be tinted with white to create soft pastels or shaded with black for a richer look.

In the morning, *there are no sleepy-heads in this cottage kitchen. Stimulating colors inspired by bold kitchen collectibles provide the visual "caffeine" that sends a wake-up call to the eyes—and spirit. Starting with dominant yellow, the owner then chose compatible analogous colors that lie next to it on the color wheel— greens, oranges, and even a dash of red. Creams and whites provide necessary visual relief, as does the cooling touch of complementary blue, which lies directly opposite orange on the color wheel that's shown at right.*

ANALOGOUS: Select three or four colors located side by side on the wheel. They can be all warm hues, all cool, or a mix.

TRIADIC: Pick any three colors that are equidistant on the wheel. Primary blue, red, and yellow are classic choices. Or, how about pale pastel lavender, peach, and green?

COMPLEMENTARY: These high-contrast palettes mix colors (such as red and green or yellow and purple) that lie opposite each other on the wheel.

START WITH YOUR FAVORITE HUE, THEN USE THE WHEEL AT RIGHT AND THE TIPS ABOVE IT TO CREATE YOUR OWN NO-FAIL COLOR PALETTE.

BEGINNING WITH BLUE

Yesterday's dull brown kitchen disappears under coats of fresh blue and white paints. To pick your own blue, start with a favorite piece of fabric, a rug, or a collectible platter or plate. Here, a hint of red mixed into the blue paint links cabinet doors to a favorite tablecloth. Painted white, a new backsplash of vintage-style beaded-board paneling adds to the cottage charm.

Maybe it has to do with sky and sea and the role they play in our fantasy getaways. Whatever the reason, blue is a color staple for creating cottage style. Besides evoking natural images that soothe the soul as well as the eye, blue carries the clout of a true classic. It's been popular so long within our homes, there are virtually no collectibles that can't be found carrying the blue banner, from blue-and-white English or Chinese pottery to old crocks with their trademark blue detailing.

Like all colors, blue affects your how you feel; it soothes your emotions and provide a sense of safety and serenity. But an all-blue scheme also can feel chilly without some warming touches. Go with cool blue and white for summer, but layer on some hot red or yellow accents when fall arrives.

Whether sponged on for a mottled effect or wiped on in subtle geometric patterns, blue paint creates a bedroom that speaks of fresh-ness and serenity. For contrast, bolder blue accents the floors and woodwork; a few yellow accents and golden woods add welcome warmth.

NATURAL EXTRACTS
—into the woods

Put yourself in Goldilocks's place and visually test the possibilities before you choose a color scheme. If vibrant multicolor schemes feel too "big" in the color department and pristine white rooms offer too little color for your taste, then the mid-range hues of the earth itself may be just right for you.

LOOK OUTSIDE FOR INSPIRATION. Take a walk across a meadow or a drive through the countryside, and you'll find your own color inspiration. It may be the barely-there color of dried wheat or cornsilk or the vibrant reds and oranges of the woods in the fall. Unlike the brash earth tones of the 1970s, today's earthy hues often look as if they were dredged up from a patch of hillside or fallen leaves.

USE COLOR FOR CHARACTER. Reminiscent of the outdoors, Mother Nature's palette, even in paint form, suggests natural textures and materials, making it a good choice when you want to create a cottage room with a rugged camp-style feeling. Paint walls a rugged russet or dark barklike taupe. Consider sponging on or combing through a second bolder color to add extra texture if your own home's walls lack the luxury of real log walls or knotty-pine or cedar paneling.

USE COLORFUL ACCENTS not only to enhance a natural-hued scheme but also to enrich it with earthy textures. Spicy-hued, a mix of nubby woven wool rugs and pillows, can lend rustic appeal.

Wheat-hued paint sets the stage for a quick lodge-style makeover. Easier to apply than the expected rough paneling and virtually as warm, the wall color teams with blanket-inspired fabrics and small accents—several birchbark canoes, a twiggy clock, and portraits of Native Americans.

Everything in this breakfast room works to underscore its natural palette: Furnishings are allowed to show off their natural beauty, and earthy fruit, plants, and baskets serve as functional accessories.

All About Earth Pigments

To find the right natural look in earth tones for your cottage palette, it may help to know a little background on the origins of color. The best hues are those closest to natural earth pigments.

■ GREENS. Green pigment can be extracted straight from nature in two different ways—through copper scrapings, or from green earth (terra verde). For the most natural look in your cottage spaces, try varying the hues; a forest consists of many shades and tints of green, not just one. ■ YELLOWS. The earth-tone examples of this color are butter, mustard, and brown yellows, not a citrus hue. Its natural pigments are ocher and raw sienna, for a flatter, older look that makes it a good color for both camp and country cottage looks. ■ REDS. These bring nature indoors when the red is a rusty brick hue, like the iron oxide that colors earth pigments.

NATURAL EXTRACTS
—earthy contrasts

In choosing your earthy palette, remember some basic color principles. Even such a subtle palette still subscribes to the same rules as any family of colors—especially those regarding the effects of warm and cool hues.

MAKE WALLS ADVANCE. Roll on a warm paint color, and your walls will seem to move toward you in a friendly, enveloping way. Warm hues may make a room appear a bit smaller—but that's not much of a price to pay for coziness.

LET WALLS RECEDE. Paint walls a cool blue or green, and they will seem to move away from you. Cool colors also create a soothing, if chilly, environment.

HAVE IT BOTH WAYS. For the best of both worlds, blend warm and cool hues, looking to your favorite outdoor settings themselves for inspiration. It's the contrast that keeps such color schemes interesting. For instance, how about the bold counterpoint of a brilliant blue sky against a yellow sand beach? Or, think of the forest in the early fall—a serene sanctuary in which the vibrant reds and yellows of changing leaves play off the greens that still remain. The country-cottage dining room shown here brings that autumn-woods color palette indoors for year-round enjoyment.

A country-lover's dream, this timeless cottage dining room gets its appeal from a rich mix of warm and cool natural colors. In paprika red, the corner cupboard and kindred checkered window swag take the edge off the cool greens. A weathered wood table contributes its own touch of warmth to the eating spot.

COTTAGE CUE. To give your own painted furnishings a more natural, weathered appearance, brush on the paint, let it dry, and then do a bit of light sanding to create a mellow, timeworn look.

PASTEL PLACES

Designing your cottage rooms in pastels is like working with cotton candy—or sherbet. It's hardly work at all. That's because pastels are among the most playful, fun-loving colors. The images they evoke are the stuff of fantasy—whether it's a Caribbean hideaway or a light-dappled cottage nestled in a meadow of wildflowers. Spin your own pastel fantasies anywhere, from bedroom to living room—and in virtually any colors you love.

PICK A HUE YOU LOVE. Except for dark neutrals, any hue in the spectrum can be expressed in a pastel: Purple becomes lavender, red becomes blush or pink, orange becomes peach, and green, yellow, and blue all lighten up into pastels, too. That's because a pastel is created simply by adding large amounts of white to a hue— the more white, the "lighter shade of pale."

ADD GRIT. Decoratively speaking, these white-tinted colors can wimp out on you unless you accent and anchor them boldly with crisp white trim, white-painted furnishings, or large-scaled furniture pieces.

The bold scale and rich patina of an antique bed adds visual strength to a potentially pallid yellow-and-white color scheme. The aged table and rocker contribute more woody warmth to the setting. Yellow walls, including a vintage-style wainscot, team with white trim and a painted checkerboard floor for cottage zip without a bit of cuteness.

Anchored by a natural fiber rug, a profusion of pillows in floral pastels adds mellow warmth to a roomful of cool white wicker. The fabrics' faded look also helps take the setting back in time.

WINDOWS WALLS FLOORS

What we call the "background"—a room's walls, floors, and windows—is much more important than its name implies. Far from passive observers of the decorating scene, these built-in surfaces and features play an integral part in creating the style and mood of your cottage design.

WINDOWS
WALLS
FLOORS

Use loosely woven or translucent fabrics when you need a treatment that adds romance while also diffusing light. Trimmed with a tasseled-flap, this fixed panel softens a street view.

Use simple cotton fabrics, such as these complementary prints, for a traditional drapery panel treatment topped by a soft swag. Note that the prints are in the same scale and color family for visual harmony. Cording adds a dressy yet understated detail to a treatment appropriate for a living or dining room. Or use one fabric for the swag and the other for the panels.

WHETHER LEFT ALONE OR SWATHED IN YARDS OF FABRIC, WINDOWS IMPART IMMEDIATE CHARACTER TO A ROOM. As you plan, start with the practical side of cottage comfort. Do you need a cover-up to filter sunlight—or to add a measure of insulation on frigid nights? Do you need privacy? Do you want to soften or screen out an anything but cottage-style view of a busy street or parking lot? Consider, too, whether you want the treatment, the window itself, or the view to dominate. For instance, a window with a garden view or one with beautifully crafted trim that's too handsome to hide may require only the simplest of treatments. Once you know your practical needs, think about your personal style, too. Imagine the crisp look of shutters, the soft romance of gathered sheers, or the farmhouse flavor of white cotton half-curtains blowing in the breeze. As you'll see in this section, you may even decide to leave well enough alone if your panes are pretty and the view is irresistible.

Contrast lining creates curtains that are simple to sew yet visually interesting. Here, the fabric gathers on tension rods for easy, no-tools installation, and panels fold back with decorative tiebacks. A 1950s-inspired print adds a lighthearted look when teamed with blue-and-white "dishtowel checks."

BETTER LEFT ALONE

With plenty of pattern already underfoot and on the pair of bamboo chairs, this living room, doesn't need yet another dose at the atrium doors. Left exposed without window treatments, the glass doors also reinforce the room's clean, fuss-free style while adding architectural impact.

Undressed and painted to contrast with the walls, these windows, also provide a serene respite from pattern while ushering in maximum light and expansive garden views. Privacy isn't needed because the windows face a courtyard.

For anyone with a heart set on decorating, windows are one temptation that's hard to resist. What a sweet invitation to introduce that favorite fabric or your brainstorm idea for whimsical hardware. But before the decorator in you takes control, stop, step back, and look around the room. If your windows are inherently charming—and, even more important, if they look out into a natural view that's worth emphasizing—they may be better left alone. Accentuate them, instead, with paint to contrast with your wall color. With no fussy fabrics to get in the way, you'll love what you see—and what you don't.

Vintage Ideas

Vintage fabrics find a new home when adapted into curtains. The same look can be created with new fabrics that look old.

■Search out old dish towels, tablecloths, and picnic napkins from family castoffs to add character to windows. ■Avoid cutting up collectible tablecloths, napkins, or hankies. Instead, drape small pieces as quick valances. You can even fold tablecloths in half and drape over a rod or thumbtack to trim. ■Recast pillowcases or dresser scarves embellished with grandma's handiwork as curtains.

 A colorful flea-market tablecloth, folded and tacked to the window trim, inspired the spirited scheme in this eye-opening breakfast room. New and old kitchen accessories pick up the bright 1940s beat. For fun, hang your own tablecloth on clothesline stretched through screw eyes.

GLANCING BACK

When a vintage character is a desired ingredient in your cottage look, put windows to work to communicate your desired sense of time and place. Salvage old or antique textiles, from tablecloths to intricate trims taken from tattered wedding gowns or handkerchiefs, to adapt to your windows.

Sheer fabric edged in delicate lace has an erstwhile look, whether or not the fabric is old. Put to service as window curtains, lace-trimmed sheers give any room a gentle refinement that smacks of the past. When used as fixed panels, lace or sheers can help you take your cottage fantasy to the limit by softening a city or suburban view.

To get started, choose old textiles that evoke the era or mood you have in mind. Cheerful, colorful patterns from the 1940s create a retro look that's popular in cottage design. For a softer, romantic mood that recalls yet an earlier generation, consider remnants of lace, cutwork, or embroidery. These white- or ivory-background pieces make their vintage statement with subtle skill, softening the room, decoratively dressing the window, and also providing privacy. If looking into the past is your goal, such lacy treatments also are ideal because they mask decidedly modern views that may lie beyond your panes.

SIMPLY PUT

There's more than one way to hang a curtain—and it's today's fresher, even quirky, alternatives that allow your own cottage style to come shining through. You already know the ordinary way: Hang the curtain with a rod running through a shirred pocket. And that's just fine, design-wise. But cottage style's fascination with the fine points—including your own personality—begs for other curtain-hanging possibilities that put more emphasis on the details, while still getting the job done neatly and simply. To find these fresh solutions, shop for:

DECORATIVE HEADERS on curtains. Tie-on tabs, smocking, and other dressmaker touches add a richly detailed look.

NEW HARDWARE and window accessories, some of which look and work like jewelry. Similar in look to a woman's brooch and in function to a workaday push pin, decorative mounts in your favorite motif simply pin curtains to the window trim, eliminating the rod. Fresh versions of classic cottage cafe rings look more like clip-on earrings, clipping ready-made curtains or plain flat fabric panels onto the rod.

GRAND FINALES, such as handsome rods, add-on finials, and fanciful supporting brackets that bring cottage chic to modern-day settings.

Charming tie-on tab curtains provide a decorating shortcut to the cottage of your dreams. Buy ready-made curtains, or simply sew flabric or ribbon tabs onto any curtain panels you like. To support the rod, wooden brackets with a painted crackle finish provide an antique look while also adding architectural presence to an ordinary room.

For star-studded curtains that are simple yet mindful of detail, stretch a panel across the window, leaving as much dip as you desire in the center. Then attach each top corner with a push-pin-style metal star mount. For a tied-back effect, pull up a bottom corner and attach it to the opposite side of the window with another star.

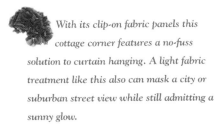

With its clip-on fabric panels this cottage corner features a no-fuss solution to curtain hanging. A light fabric treatment like this also can mask a city or suburban street view while still admitting a sunny glow.

GRACEFUL FORMS

Ah, romance....If you lean toward the softer side of cottage style, choose window dressings that are graceful but not elaborate—feminine without being fussy. Because the solution lies in soft, shapely designs created by light and simple fabrics that easily billow and puff, you can enjoy this romance without a major commitment of decorating dollars.

Even the name "balloon shade" has a playful sound. Whether gathered, pleated, or even smocked at the top, these fabric dressings fall into balloon-like poufs at the bottom to bring childlike charm to any room. Raised by cords threaded through rings, balloon shades pull up to let the sun—and the view—shine in.

CREATE LUSH GATHERS, instead of skimpy curtains that fall flat, by making sure that your curtain panels measure at least two—and preferably three—times your window's width. To keep such full curtains from blocking the view or sunlight when pulled open, consider mounting them on a rod that's wider than the window.

BUY OR HEM EXTRA-LONG CURTAINS so they fall into soft puddles on the floor. Because the most graceful puddles can be formed with low-cost sheer fabric, such curtains can captivate the eye without gobbling up the budget.

ADD A PUFFY BALLON SHADE or balloon-style valance to soften existing blinds or shades. To pouf up a stationary balloon valance, tuck in a few wads of scrunched-up tissue paper.

An inherently rugged, wood-paneled bathroom may not seem the most likely candidate for a tie-back curtain swag that puddles at the floor. But then again, why not? Inspired by a beach house, this delightful getaway-style bath reflects cottage style's blend of romance with natural, even rugged materials.

Give shape to a corner window wall by tying back sheer panels toward each other. Gathering the panels tightly, instead of stretching them out across the full width of the windows, creates a fuller, more feminine look. A wide, floppy ruffle adds more shape at the edges.

WINDOWS
WALLS
FLOORS

Turn to wallpaper to add cottage charm to any room. Here, a lattice design sets an airy garden mood in a small bath. Cottage designs include everything from simple stripes and fanciful florals to adorable teapots.

Whether clad in wide planks like these or ordinary plaster, walls and trim gain both serenity and coziness when painted a rich deep green. If walls aren't in pristine condition, use a flat-finish paint to minimize flaws—or a semigloss for a subtle touch of shine.

CREATIVE COLORS AND FINISHES CAN HELP YOU HARNESS THE DECORATING POWER OF YOUR ROOM'S LARGEST SURFACES, ITS WALLS. With cottage design's emphasis on the personal style, the only "rule" is that you should select wall colors or patterns by design, not by default. For example, crisp white drywall, when deliberately chosen, can set the perfect tone for a pared-down cottage scheme—but it will fall flat if your goal is English cottage romance. To acquaint you with some of the possibilities, this section includes paint treatments that declare the palette, decorative paintwork that offers a friendly handcrafted look, wallpapers or fabrics that wrap rooms in cottage motifs, and a range of panelings, from old-style beadboard to unexpected corrugated tin.

Crisp and neutral stripes can create a romantic look or a bright and breezy one, depending on their color and the context in which they're used. Tape off the wall and paint in your choice of white and a bright or two shades of the same color. Or even easier, find a striped wallpaper in the color and width that works for you. Here, touches of pine, lace, and farm-fresh accents add romance.

STRIPED, STAMPED, AND STENCILED

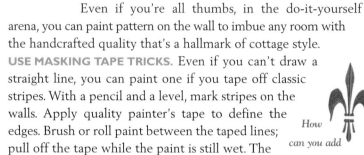

Even if you're all thumbs, in the do-it-yourself arena, you can paint pattern on the wall to imbue any room with the handcrafted quality that's a hallmark of cottage style.

USE MASKING TAPE TRICKS. Even if you can't draw a straight line, you can paint one if you tape off classic stripes. With a pencil and a level, mark stripes on the walls. Apply quality painter's tape to define the edges. Brush or roll paint between the taped lines; pull off the tape while the paint is still wet. The palette? How about blue or yellow stripes over pure white for beach-house breeziness? Or, for a softer look, paint taupe stripes over a cream-white base. You can mix materials, too. For farmhouse chic, cover the lower third of a wall with white beaded-board paneling and then stripe the wall above it.

STENCIL ON SOME STYLE. Stencils blend ready-made pattern with the chance to select colors to match favorite fabrics, rugs, or linens. How about a stenciled "chair rail" of snappy checks, a frieze of flowers, or twining ivy to frame a bed? Use painter's tape to hold the stencil in place, then start dabbing. A nearly dry brush is the key to avoiding runs and bleeding edges.

STAMP ON A PATTERN. A scattering of simple hearts or diamonds can transform a bland wall in a flash. Just practice your technique on cardboard before trying it on the wall. Don't worry about getting the same amount of paint or ink on every stamped image; subtle variations add handcrafted appeal and the imprint of personality.

How can you add cottage charm to a bland room and a ho-hum sofa? Join two decorative paint treatments together at the walls for tactile appeal and hand-painted warmth. Here, the painted stripes add vertical thrust and a look of depth. Simply stamped on top of the stripes, fleur-de-lis designs add another rich layer and a dose of playfulness. For depth and contrast, vary paint finishes; over flat-painted walls, use gloss paint for stencils. A skirted table, a soft throw, and lace curtains lend more romance and rich texture.

Whether you're stamping, stenciling, or brushing on some stripes, consider the effect that the paint finish will have on your design. For a soft and subtle look, use flat-finish paint for both the base coat and the motifs that you paint over it. In contrast, use gloss paint (such as acrylic enamel) over flat walls for depth and drama.

SPECIAL EFFECTS

In addition to applying pattern to the walls, special decorative paint treatments can apply a soothing balm to your psyche when they're planned with a twist of trickery in mind. Where do you want to "go" after a hard day? If, for example, a stone cottage in the country is your dream, why not surround yourself with walls painted to replicate aged stonework? Or how about escaping into the past with the layered look of timeworn plaster? Start with your own dream, then consider how to make it happen. Illusory paint treatments take one of three forms.

FAUX FINISHES mimic a material, such as marble or wood, in paint. Some are easier than others. For a faux stone wall, sponge on two or three mottled, stony hues, let dry, then paint contrasting "mortar lines" to outline "blocks."

TROMPE L'OEIL refers to a painted scene created by an artist to convincingly replicate an object on a wall or on a piece of furniture. Trompe l'oeil and many faux finishes require the hand of a true artist; contact galleries or art schools for recommendations.

SPONGING AND COLOR-WASHING (and similar techniques, such as using plastic dry cleaner's bags for daubing paint on and off), give the appearance of dimension or age to a wall. And they're easy for amateurs to master. Enrich your walls by sponging on two or more colors inspired by your favorite fabrics. Use a natural sea sponge for the softest patterns, and let one coat dry before applying another.

Special finishes impart a sense of age. Faux-finish baseboards trim off a trompe l'oeil design that imitates an aging outdoor garden wall in Tuscany. Earthenware urns put the walls' new-found touch of texture and antiquity into three-dimensional form.

Are they marble or are they paint? Who cares? The faux-marble finish on these crown moldings takes this ceiling back in time. The handpainted finish also ages the room by suggesting the crafts-manship of the past.

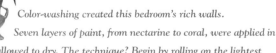

Color-washing created this bedroom's rich walls. Seven layers of paint, from nectarine to coral, were applied in turn and allowed to dry. The technique? Begin by rolling on the lightest hue. Apply each subsequent coat with thinner, more watered-down paint, using cotton rags and a scrubbing motion to allow previous coats to show through. The variegated design creates the aged look.

COTTAGE ROOM WRAPS
—paper assets

Fresh and informal, warm and friendly, cottage walls can quickly create whatever kind of getaway mood you have in mind. Success comes in deciding whether you want the walls to play a starring or supporting role in your decorating scheme. If you're unsure, ask yourself, "Does my room have any decorating guts?" Look around. If your walls and furnishings seem nondescript—if they don't convey cottage spirit—it's time to start building cottage character in one of two ways.

EMPHASIZE COTTAGE FURNISHINGS. If your dreams of a cottage getaway include an eye-grabbing four-poster, an imposing armoire, or even folk art pieces, play them up with subtly colored or textured wall coverings. This is also true if your home has rugged exposed beams or shapely windows to which you want to call attention.

LET THE WALLS STAR. If you can't look at a room without envisioning the major role that wallpaper can play in its decorating drama, don't fight the feeling. Let a colorful teapot patterned wallpaper border or, perhaps, a beautifully flowered wall covering inspire your entire room scheme.

Choose fabric and wall covering patterns at the same time so they can work as equal patterns to wrap a room in cozy color. Here, the patterns are color-keyed, but neither dominates. For a quick faux canopy, use toggle bolts to anchor a wooden frame to the ceiling, then gather and staple fabric to the outside of the frame. Conceal the staples with glued-on trim. Create wall and bed curtains by stapling fabric or by shirring rod-pocket panels onto rods affixed inside the frame and on the wall.

With its celestial colors and pattern, this dappled cottage wallpaper provides dreamy background music. The paper adds charm by mimicking sponge painting, yet it doesn't upstage the room's starring canopy bed with its lacy topper and antique quilt.

Against the Wall

Do your walls leave you feeling, well, flat? Add some zip with cottage textures.

■ Break up boxiness instantly with a floor screen. Screens of fabric, wood, bifold doors, or metal will set the mood you want while hiding anything from unsightly radiators to a private mini home office. Or, how about hinging together three or four actual screen doors to underscore a porchlike theme? ■ Garden latticework applied directly over the walls sets a breezy mood. Paint it a different color from the wall for contrast, or let it blend for subtlety. ■ For a country cottage scene, nail white picket fencing over the lower third of a wall.

The farm shed look of corrugated tin imparts rustic character and wit to this dining room. Shiny and sleek, the tin also serves as a tactile counterpoint to the wood furnishings and primitives.

COTTAGE ROOM WRAPS

—fresh textures

Inspired by cottage style's invent-as-you-go playfulness, sheets and other fabric panels turn up in unlikely places. Hang them on the wall as romantic accents or from the ceiling to divide space. Here, fabric drapes swag-style from star mounts to turn a once dull corner into an inviting spot for a writing table or a makeup vanity. And changing the decor is as easy as pinning up fresh sheets!

If plain painted walls are not for you, look beyond traditional wall coverings and consider some creative, character-adding alternatives. While wallpaper may be the surest way to envelop a room in pattern and color, it's not the only option. Simply textured materials can create a getaway mood while either camouflaging damaged walls or taking the cold edge off brand-new ones.

LOG OR PINE PANELING quickly turns a city or new dry suburban den into a "mountain retreat."

OLD-STYLE BEADED-BOARD PANELING injects vintage farmhouse character into any space.

CORRUGATED TIN adds a fun farmyard feeling that's just right if you love folk art and primitive furnishings.

SOFT FABRIC, whether shirred on rods, gathered on Shaker-style pegs, or stapled on smoothly, romances any space.

WINDOWS
WALLS
FLOORS

With its random-width planks and satiny finish, new oak flooring lends antique character to a redone attic. The dark oak also shows off the rug's nubby texture and intricate patterns.

Go beyond standard strip oak if wood is your choice. Here, wide-plank pine, with visible knots, adds to the cozy charm of a living room. Don't worry about the inevitable dents and dings that new pine floors suffer. That natural aging is part of the charm. Wood floors also give you the opportunity to show off colorful accents rugs, such as this lattice-patterned design, which are key elements in creating cottage style. Other rug possibilities? Hooked, braided, needlepoint, and woven cottons.

WHETHER YOUR COTTAGE STYLE IS BARE AND SPARE OR FILLED WITH RUFFLES AND FLOURISHES, USE YOUR FLOOR COVERINGS TO ENHANCE IT. To put your floors to work, first be sure the texture suits you. Do you prefer the softness of carpet or the sleek feel of well-waxed wood? Consider, too, the role that pattern should play in your scheme. For instance, if your decorating attitude is light-hearted, why not play it up with a whimsical painted floor or area rug? Think, too, about where you want to put your emphasis. A pattern-free floor of wood or sisal will keep the focus on a great furniture piece or a view. However, if your room is a bland box, the view is so-so, or your furnishings are less than exciting, why not grab your eye with romantic floral carpet? This section will help you envision the right choice for your style and your room.

Brick pavers or brick-shaped quarry tiles bring the charm of a garden path indoors. Naturally beautiful, they also make carefree hosts for indoor plants and watering cans.

FOOLERY UNDERFOOT

Stop treating your floors like, well, doormats. Sure, they obligingly let you walk all over them, but can't they have a little fun, too? The same just-for-fun artistry that your walls enjoy can give your floors their own moments in the spotlight. In fact, with the right painted designs, these hardworking surfaces can become peers with other furnishings—equal participants in creating your room's fresh cottage-style sparkle and snap. Here are some tips.

Because they are floors, these surfaces merit a different kind of fool-the-eye scene than is found on the walls. Most often, it's some version of a painted-on area rug that mimics anything from a bed of flowers to a fish-filled pond. Whether your canvas consists of aging sheet vinyl, real wood, plywood, or a movable canvas floorcloth, colorful and quick-drying acrylic paints—protected by coats of nonyellowing polyurethane—can create any scene you like.

Such trompe l'oeil rugs are functional, too—a practical solution for high-traffic or wet spaces off-limits to real rugs. They also save money if you paint simple designs yourself. If the floor is in down-at-the-heels shape, this decorative solution conceals years of scuff marks, scratches, and stains with a cottage-style dash of humor.

A stroll in the garden is cheerily evoked by a flower-bed scene on this cottage sunroom floor. An intricate design like this may require a pro, but don't be shy about painting a simpler design on the floor or on a canvas floor cloth. To paint your own floor cloth, buy primed canvas and acrylic paints at an art or crafts store. Mark off simple checks or a trellis design with artist's masking tape, then brush or stencil on your pattern. Let the canvas dry, then protect it with a coat or two of nonyellowing polyurethane.

This kitchen's plaid floor was created by first applying a base coat of white, then measuring out the design's lines with a straightedge and marking them off with painter's masking tape. A mix of solid and sponged colors creates the special effects.

Finding Room To Paint a Rug

A custom-designed, painted-on area rug adds individual character as it pulls together a room's palette. Paint a design on wood, on vinyl, or on a ready-made canvas floor cloth sold at art stores.

■ Paint a trompe l'oeil area rug after a fabric or wallpaper used in the same room to knit the space together through palette and pattern. ■ Bring a smile to your hearth: Paint an area rug there, replete with a depiction of the family pet snoozing in front of the fire. Or, have a local artist or art student do the work. ■ Instead of carpeting time-worn wooden stairs, transform them with a painted-on runner in your favorite cottage colors and motifs. ■ All thumbs? Rely on stencils, or use artist's tape to define simple geometric designs. ■ Accent a porch with a "rug" that needn't come inside when it rains. Sand the wood floor, and paint a small rug to anchor a sitting spot. How about bright freehand fish swimming in a sea of blue?

SOFT TOUCH

Painted-on pattern creates visual magic underfoot; but when a soft touch is called for, nothing tickles your toes like the textures of the real thing. Wall-to-wall carpet provides the desired sink-down softness. But unless your carpet is a patterned floral or lattice design, it probably doesn't go far enough to convey cottage style. That's where area rugs come in. Here's how to choose and use one.

Even in humble cottage style, bathrooms serve as the luxurious retreats of the home. It only makes sense that they become invested with some of the same sensuous trappings of other spaces—inevitably, area rugs. This needlepoint floral brings delicate grace to a romantic cottage bath.

PICK A PATTERN AND A PALETTE that project your room's style. Do you dream of a walk in the garden? The cozy look of great-grandma's braided designs? The outdoorsy feeling of natural, wheat-hued sisal or rush matting? Or the bold beachy look of snappy cabana stripes? Needlepoint area rugs lend a romantic cottage feeling; hooked or braided rugs are good choices for a farmhouse cottage flavor.

LET THE RUG LEAD YOUR EYE to special furniture groupings or architectural features. Yes, it's fine to lay a rug right over your carpet to accent a fireplace, anchor a dining table, or add softness at bedside. Or, place the rug under a coffee table to unify a sofa and chairs. And don't forget the kitchen or bath. A cotton rug can add a dash of color and pattern yet be whisked away for laundering.

In love with English cottages? Use a rug that scatters delicate bouquets on the floor, then echo the feeling with color-keyed floral fabrics on some pillows and an ottoman.

 In this cottage living room, wall-to-wall carpet retains a neutral role while adding earthy texture underfoot. However, it's the natural rug laid on top of the carpet beneath the coffee table that defines the conversation area while also adding an extra measure of wheatlike color and texture to the setting.

STENCILED STYLE

As an achievable do-it-yourself project, decorative stenciling has few peers. It's manageable even by the homeowner who can't draw a straight line. An ability to dab paint is really all you need to spruce up a floor.

Stenciled patterns can be a lifesaver for has-been floors. Old wooden boards that seem beyond redemption with too many scars of age manage to last another lifetime beneath stenciled-on paint. Though there are many specific patterns and applications, the two basic varieties of stencils are geometric and figurative. In selecting one of the two types for your floor, seek a balance with other patterns in the room:

Delicate shading can add depth to a border. Here, the cheery colors and soft swirls of the border also take the hard edge off the green-and-white grid.

WALK A FINE LINE with a geometric stencil if your room already is filled with floral fabrics and wall coverings. The linear strength of a checked floor stencil can provide just the grounding that such a room needs.

ADD A CURVY TOUCH. A figurative stenciled rug or a border of flowers or ivy will add shapely contrast and relief to a room that suffers from too many hard edges created by its furnishings or its geometric fabric and wall covering designs.

GET THE BEST OF BOTH and decorate your floor in a stenciled treatment that combines the geometric with the figurative. How about an ivy border around a painted checkerboard rug or a checked border around a field of flowers?

When applied with classic quilts in mind, exterior stains in barn red, gray blue, whitewash, and golden oak bring vibrant cottage spirit to any porch or deck. Make trianglular stencils, or mask off triangles; apply stains. Protect the finish with at least two coats of a nonyellowing polyurethane.

CHOOSE THE RIGHT PAINT. Consider acrylic enamel, which comes in dozens of colors and dries quickly, or translucent wood stains, which offer color yet allow some wood grain to show. Both require polyurethane protection. Special floor paints are durable but not usually desirable for decorating projects because they come in a limited range of hues.

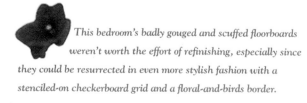

This bedroom's badly gouged and scuffed floorboards weren't worth the effort of refinishing, especially since they could be resurrected in even more stylish fashion with a stenciled-on checkerboard grid and a floral-and-birds border.

ARTFUL ACCENTS

With your backgrounds, furnishings, and fabrics in place, you're off to a good start in creating cottage style for your home. But the real fun is yet to come. It lies in the final touches—those decorative accents, be they art or another kind of accessory—that bring your rooms one-of-a-kind character by revealing your own personality.

Architectural Finds

Use the following tips to turn architectural remnants into decorative accessories that work hard, too.

■ For a slim hall table or a dining room serving and display spot, mount a pair of old corbels on the wall, then top with glass. ■ Top an architectural capital (the top of a column) with glass for new life as an endtable. ■ Turn the newel post from an antique staircase into a plant stand. ■ Soften a corner or subdivide space with the architectural impact of a floor screen made of antique doors hinged together. ■ Recycle a curlicued iron gate as a romantic headboard.

SALVAGED ARCHITECTURE

The same beautifully crafted architectural elements that brought charm to the buildings of yesteryear can breathe fresh life into cottage interiors when used as decorative accessories. Use an entire collection of architectural remnants—say, Victorian garden accents—to thematically unite a room. Or, let a single remnant, such as a vintage fireplace surround, surprise an otherwise contemporary space. The fun is in the act of discovering such treasures and looking at their potential uses with a fresh eye. Consider the possibilities of fancifully carved corbels, turned newel posts or balusters, or classical columns and their capitals (the upper section that tops the column post). Or, imagine the charm that you can give your rooms with scraps of Victorian gingerbread trim, iron fencing or gates, or beautifully shaped antique windows.

An artful collage of mismatched architectural remnants crowns this fireplace. Salvaged shutters, hinged to form a floor screen, soften a corner while balancing the height of the mantel treatment. Perched atop worn posts, old birdhouses bring a smile. Even the kitchen table, cut down and placed by the sofa, sends a relaxed message.

Be creative when shopping for architectural remnants. A single bold element, such as a weathered newel post, can make a sculptural cottage accent.

Vestiges of our architectural past instantly give any room a bit of nostalgia. Cottage-style seekers can find everything from bas-relief carvings of classical motifs to fancy carved finials at specialty shops displaying wares salvaged from old houses and buildings.

Truly Tiny Gardens

Instead of the usual vase or pot to hold flowers or plants, invent your own receptacle from other everyday objects.

■ Clear-glass salad dressing cruets in staggered sizes make sweet bud vases, especially when massed together for maximum impact. ■ Collect old glass milk bottles for wild-flower centerpieces; display them together in an old wood or metal milk crate. ■ Let small bouquets nestle into your cupboard's usually hidden assets, such as creamers and gravy bowls. ■ To work needed height into a tabletop grouping, recycle olive oil bottles (or any other tall glass vessels) to hold tall blooms, grasses, or twigs.

Birdhouses make friendly companions for houseplants on a wire stand or shelf. To keep the eye moving, the bird abodes are interspersed with plants, instead of being displayed all in a row.

GARDEN GROWTH

With a bit of fresh greenery or just-clipped flowers, you can enrich any cottage look, from the most rugged camp style to the most decorative English cottage design.

LET FLOWERS ENTERTAIN YOU. The same room can take on casual or formal airs, depending on the occasion. Freshly cut flowers casually plopped in a bell jar or a pitcher create a relaxed cottage feeling that's just right for casual gatherings. Planning a fancier affair? Arrange stems more carefully in a treasured cut-glass vase for a more formal look, or frame a mantel with topiaries. Opt for old-fashioned roses to conjure up romance—or carefree daisies and wildflowers for a looser look.

BRING COTTAGE DETAILS INSIDE. Love exterior window boxes? Bring the look inside. Mount the real thing beneath an indoor window sill, or gather flowering plants or herbs on a stand set before a sunny window. Add water, too; float candles in a shapely, water-filled birdbath displayed on a year-round porch, or buy a mini indoor fountain for the sound of running water all year long.

This spot uses plant life to carry out its neoclassical slant on cottage style—a look begun by its architectural coffee table. A dresser gains focal-point status when paired it with a wall-hung mirror and symmetrically placed topiaries. An armful of roses left unexpectedly in a basket says as much about the style's spontaneity as it does about its quest for garden freshness.

A FULL PLATE

Whether new or old, plates decorated with delicate, old-fashioned patterns add a comforting look to any would-be room. No wonder plates are one of the collectibles especially conducive to creating cottage style. Many plates are based on centuries-old blue-and-white Chinese designs, but even new hand-painted china plates can convey the same look and mood. Or consider the folk-art appeal and bold palette of French Quimper ware. All of the plates need not be the same pattern. In fact, it's the mix of motifs and sizes that creates coveted, collected-over-time appeal. To put your plates on parade:

HANG A SLIM PLATE RACK for a colorful and space-efficient cottage accent. A kitchen or dining area wall makes an obvious spot, but don't overlook the cozy effect that a plate-filled rack can have on a bedroom, living room, or den.

CHARM A TABLETOP OR A SHELF by displaying your favorite handpainted plate upright on its own miniature easel.

RIM A ROOM with a palette-pleasing frieze of plates hung at the ceiling line.

PUT DECORATIVE PLATES IN ORBIT by arranging them so they surround a painting or a wall-hung clock.

Turn skinny strip of kitchen space into a canvas for cottage style by hanging a row of pretty plates vertically on a wall or on the side of a cabinet. The different patterns and sizes increase the visual interest.

The blue-and-white color scheme of this living room is repeated in the details—a collection of four plates taken straight to the windows and displayed on the frames of the lower sashes. Placement of two plates on the two outer panes of a pair of windows creates symmetrical balance; the two windows appear as mirror images. An off-center topiary grouped with a bunny, a birdhouse, and a scattering of porcelain treasures keeps the look cottage-casual by breaking up any hint of rigid symmetry.

A collection of patterned plates of varying sizes and designs becomes the focal point of a dining room wall when the plates are mounted in a circular configuration around a clock. This arrangement features radial balance, meaning that all the pieces radiate out from a central point.

CANNED GOODS

Old watering cans gain new personality when painted in Easter-egg colors. For harmony, the pretty pastels share the same color value and intensity. Multi-colored cans provide more visual continuity, because the accent colors used on one repeat the main color featured on another.

Garden themes are a sure way of conveying cottage style quickly, both indoors and out. Over recent years, one humble object—the old tin watering can—has risen to prominence as a garden element worthy of decorative function. New tin replicas abound, but if you're in the market for the real, weathered thing, be aware that it may take some browsing to find a good deal. Still, if you want to communicate cottage style, old garden implements are worth the effort and expense. Massed together on an old bench, they bring the idea of puttering in the garden indoors. And, if displayed on a porch or deck, they give visitors an enticing preview of your cottage style.

Smile!

Assembled together on a weathered bench, freshly painted watering cans sporting primary colors declare a cheery cottage-style greeting upon entry to this home.

PERSONAL TOUCH

Forget scouring the stores for the perfect cottage accessories. A little soul-searching will bring you closer to the look you want. Think about your hobbies and interests, then about the special equipment, books, awards, or clothing they entail. Chances are, you already own the most meaningful accessories for your home but haven't thought of using them as such. Ski poles, tennis rackets, snowshoes, riding tack, fly rods—all express who you are, and all can be put to use decorating your rooms with the most personal of cottage styles.

TELL YOUR STORY. Bring photos out of the closet; display them as tabletop art.

FRAME THE FUNK. Attic finds, such as old sheet music, 1920s magazine covers, and children's art, personalize walls.

DRESS UP by hanging collected hats, ties, and costume jewelry in artfully composed groupings to give your rooms a distinctive handprint.

Decorating with what you love—and only what you love—opens the door not only to heartfelt personal style but offers a surprising bonus: Stress reduction. By ferreting out those things that have special meaning (and ditching the rest), you can actually clear a path to a more serene, less cluttered way of living.

A bedroom vanity table becomes a haven for one-of-a-kind style when you layer it with a nostalgic blend of white table dressings, matching silver champagne glasses filled with roses, and favorite colognes and toiletries. A romantic bonus, the wall mirror hangs by a wide ribbon.

Grouping your favorite things in one spot brings heartwarming style to any tabletop, especially when objects include personal photographs. This mix blends a trip down memory lane with eye-pleasing diversity of texture, from the rough grapevine wreath to the smooth glass lamp. The wreath also serves to balance the height and size of the lamp.

In cottage style, the more personal the details, the better, as this living room tabletop proves. A swarm of small framed family photos recounts the past and relates a story of personal history that brings warmth better than any finery.

Let the Lobster who never loved m
Now love me, and love me mo

THE NATURALS

Treats to the eye and to the soul, objects found in nature—and the special accessories made from them—can bring the spirit of your favorite getaway inside. Their presence on a tabletop, a bench, or a bedside not only complements cottage style's embrace of the open air but also simplifies all that's around with a casual, can't-be-faked realness.

WHAT'S YOUR DREAM? Natural treasures, from pinecones to seashells, offer instant relaxation, transporting you to the woods or the beach in just a glance.

CREATE MINI "LANDSCAPES." In an open box, basket, or on a small wooden tray, group kindred objects from the same natural place. Rocks, moss, and leaves recall a walk in the woods; sand, shells, and even a miniature deck chair for fun suggest a day at the beach.

LAYER IN OR UNDER GLASS. Arrange pretty leaves under newly cut glass on an endtable or a vanity. Or layer finds, such as river rocks or acorns, in a tall clear vase or open jar for high drama.

LET LARGER ITEMS SOLO. Think of a shell, a piece of driftwood, a shapely rock, or a hunk of colorful quartz as "sculpture" for a mantel or a coffee table.

Pine needle baskets bristle with outdoor presence, also reflecting a nearly lost craft that artisans are reviving today.

A single starfish holds its own in this tabletop still life composed of natural objects— roses, rocks, grapes, and a shell-art box. Smooth porcelain and glass play off beautifully against the wicker, shells, and rough wood.

COTTAGE CUE. Use a natural touch on a table or two and see what happens. Keep objects exactly as they are now, then add one bold seashell, rock, driftwood, or any other treasure from your own favorite faraway place.

LIVING ROOMS

Something strange happens in the cottage living room—people actually live in it! Whether your personal decorating style is romantic, porchy, or Provençal, count on comfortable sink-in seating and plenty of ottomans to ensure a casual, feet-up atmosphere that will welcome your family and guests alike.

Building The Circle

When comfort counts, how you arrange your furnishings is actually more important than the pieces themselves. Here's how to cozy up your living room.

■ Decide on a focal point—a strong, visually engaging element that forms a natural magnet for gatherings. Yours may be a fireplace, a hutch, a bank of windows, or an oversize painting. In the room at right, French doors form one focal point; a fireplace lies out of view at the left. ■ Group seating around the focus, anchoring the circle with a sofa and angling chairs to clip the corners. ■ Create a secondary anchor (and a spot for your favorite cottage things) with an ample coffee or tea table. ■ Place small tables, ottomans, and lamps next to seating pieces for cottage ease. ■ Include cozy and practical lamplight as part of the sitting spot, then dot other lamps, such as picture lights and strip lights for shelves, around the room for a nighttime glow.

CIRCLE OF FRIENDS

When you pull pieces into a snug circle, you make space around the edges for satellite groupings that add function while delighting the eye. How about a chair plus a small library table or desk—or simply a rocker and a floor lamp for some solo rocking and reading?

In the cottage living room, family, friends—and furnishings—gather into intimate, informal groupings. The right furnishings and arrangement can give this convivial core of the home both a friendly, feel-good atmosphere for the family and enough snap and polish for receiving guests. To make your own living room serve both functions:

START WITH THE CLASSICS. Roll-arm sofas and chairs—overstuffed, of course—add comfort as well as style.

PULL SEATING IN from the walls for a close-knit conversation spot placing people no more than 8 feet apart.

GO NATURAL. Warm woods, roughly textured wicker, or barklike rattan will underscore a room's new, cottage-fresh ambience.

ANCHOR THE SITTING SPOT with a sofa placed so its back directs traffic around the circle; bring in a couple of armchairs, angling them inward for coziness.

ADD A CENTRAL FOCUS with a coffee or tea table large enough to hold books and photos plus guests' teacups—or that just-delivered pizza!

WORK IN SOME TALL PIECES as you arrange the other furniture. Lofty bookcases or armoires carry the eye upward.

Decorating doesn't get any easier than this. White walls and bare windows form an airy backdrop for cushy roll-arm seating that's clad in no-fail cottage classics: stripes and florals. Pulled away from the walls into a snug circle, the floating island is anchored securely by both an area rug and a generously sized coffee table. Flowers, family photos, and a flock of birdhouses add just the right touch of personality.

COTTAGE CUE. Don't let your cottage style go flat on the coffee table. As you arrange your favorite things—books, a trio of treasured teacups or whatever you love—add vertical interest with at least one tall object, such as a vase, an upright plate rack, or even a birdhouse.

KEEPING TRADITION

The informal, low-pile area rug and clean, patternless walls create a breezy cottage canvas for this living room's traditional furniture shapes. Oversized wicker chairs also add a touch of relaxation to the tight-back, roll-arm sofa and eighteenth-century-style cocktail table.

A cottage feeling abides in this living room where clean-scrubbed pale walls and airy, informal sheers and blinds lighten up traditional pieces of dark, polished wood. Using light-colored and minimally patterned upholstery fabrics and pine accent furnishings helps banish any potential feeling of formality.

If you love cottage coziness but your taste runs to beloved furniture classics rooted in the eighteenth century, take heart: You *can* have it both ways. In the cottage living room there's always room for traditional furniture as long as pieces are lightened up with more casual decorative elements.

To keep formal fussiness at bay, start with a clean and simple background. Consider painting the walls a light neutral color or white to convey an airy, cottage feeling. White shutters, unadorned shades, or plain curtain panels also create a casual attitude. Avoid window treatments that are elaborately shaped, formally trimmed, or made of heavy fabrics, such as tapestries and brocades. Next, add a few rustic or rough-textured furnishings to offset the formality of your traditional pieces. Even mahogany fits in well when it is neighbored with informal pieces, such as a single primitive pine bench, a painted folk-art chest, or a casual wicker chair. Finally, bring your space together by letting furnishings snuggle up to an area rug, whether neutral and natural or colorfully patterned.

COLLECTIBLE CACHET

Even a plain-vanilla room can take on cottage charm when you bring in a few folkish and fun objects. In fact, neutral walls and upholstery make a perfect canvas for an ever-changing array of just-found treasures. What kinds of objects and arrangements naturally draw your eye? Do you gravitate toward boldly displayed folk art? Or do little things, from teacups to delicate trims on pillows, mean a lot to you? Whatever your treasures, for decorative impact be sure to cluster small objects and to leave ample "air" around larger ones.

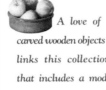

A love of carved wooden objects links this collection that includes a model ship and an antique fish weather vane gathered to create a focal point. To display such large, sculptural objects, leave breathing room around each one, and balance high and low objects. In this room, the birdhouses in the center and on the side wall lead the eye in a graceful, rhythmic dip.

When gathered into one spot, pillows decorated with vintage buttons and lace add cottage charm versus clutter. Smaller collectibles, such as pillows, perfume bottles, candlesticks, and framed photos, create decorating drama when displayed en masse instead of individually.

LIGHT AND BREEZY

Light pastel walls and simply chic Roman shades set an airy summer-house theme. With their curvaceous shapes and wicker construction, ample armchairs lend comfort without appearing heavy. Floral fabric, instead of a bulky solid, minimizes the visual weight of the sofa in the foreground.

Big comfort can take on a light-and-breezy cottage look when you put your major furnishings and surfaces on a "decorating diet." **USE A SLIMMING PALETTE OF LIGHT HUES** to reduce the visual weight of oversized, sink-in sofas and chairs. Even large, solid surfaces, such as walls and floors, look airier when dressed in pale colors. **LOOK FOR OPEN FURNITURE DESIGNS** to add lightness. Tables with see-through bases and chairs with exposed legs assume a lighter look than same-sized pieces with more enclosed designs. **FOR BREEZY SOFTNESS,** create a fluid visual flow with fabrics, wood trim, and wicker that offer curving patterns and lines. **LEAVE WINDOWS UNCOVERED** to forge a connection between your room and the outdoors. Or, dress them in sheers to combine a bit of day-long privacy with a sunny glow.

A pint-size room opens up with minimal pattern and pale neutrals that allow upholstery to blend into the walls and windows. The open coffee table and wicker bench keep the look light. Beautifully clustered, the toss pillows and the artful array on the end-table lend homey style without fussiness.

OF THE EARTH

Textures give this sunny living space a relaxed, earthy feeling. A gardenlike rattan table and sofa mix easily with primitive oak pressed-back chairs, porch-style window shades, and a bounty of potted plants. Even the traditional, cabriole-legged chair and ottoman can relax when clad in casual plaid and set atop a natural rug.

Forget what you may have heard. It's Mother—well, Mother Nature, anyway—who knows best, at least when it comes to creating naturally appealing and relaxing living rooms. When casual cottage style is your goal, turn to natural textures—things with a woolly, rough, or nubby feel—in both furnishings and floor coverings. To set your own degree of informality, remember that the rougher the texture, the more casual the look. (Envision, for instance, the formal look of polished mahogany versus the casual feeling of rough-hewn pine.) By limiting the use of slick, smooth textures associated with formal fabrics and finishes in favor of more earthy materials, you also can give a casual twist to traditional furniture. Even Queen Anne chairs with graceful cabriole legs ease up when teamed with a rough sisal rug and a weathered iron table.

White paneling lends fresh-and-friendly front-porch ambience to what could have been a formal space. Against that tactile backdrop, a traditional roll-arm easy chair becomes cottage-worthy when dressed casually and paired with an earthy wicker chair. Dark finishes and checked fabrics are the visual ties that bind the mismatched chairs. Mellow mixers—the sisal rug, baskets, and a cut-down wooden work-bench used as a coffee table—reinforce the room's casual look.

FOLK ART FOR FUN

This living room's bookshelves and sofa are definitively contemporary— a perfect, sleek foil for finely crafted collectibles. The collection of folk art, given the attention it deserves in special niches, is all that's needed to thoroughly articulate the cottage-style statement. The whimsical folk-art toys are sure to bring a smile.

Airy white walls, wicker, pine, and stripes create an outdoor atmosphere that's perfect for showcasing a flock of birdhouses that are grouped to draw and delight the eye.

With their droll wit, informal styling, and naive handmade character, folk-art collectibles bring the spirit of cottage style to virtually any living room. In fact, because handmade folk art almost instantly relaxes formality and adds friendliness to a room, adding just a piece or two will start the transition of your living room to cottage style. In addition to offering cottage charm, folk art adds a measure of soul, warming a living room with the presence of the artist's personality.

The whimsical, rustic nature of folk art makes a personal statement about you, too, so let your taste—and budget—be your guide.

IF YOU'RE A CONNOISSEUR seeking investment pieces, as well as stylish ones, consider antique folk-art dolls and toys, which are among the most amusing and valuable pieces. Look for familiar items that will remind you of your own childhood—or that of your parents or grandparents.

IF YOU'RE NOT A SERIOUS COLLECTOR of antique, museum-quality pieces, visit crafts fairs, galleries, and boutiques where you'll find a bumper crop of delightful, affordable new offerings created by today's talented folk artists. Popular choices in plentiful supply include birdhouses and decoys.

Either way, display just a few thoughtfully chosen folk art pieces in gallerylike fashion to make a contemporary cottage statement.

Birdhouses of a feather stick together. Here, rough wood bird abodes hang out on a low shelf, while a pristine white birdhouse goes it alone on the tabletop. Like the birdhouses, the flowering plants and fabrics help link the room with the garden that lies just outside the windows.

On the table: CREATIVE PAINTING WITH PASTEL

ROMANTIC REMAKE

A mix of neutral, patternless seating pieces, whether new or newly reupholstered, creates serenity. Here, such pieces step graciously into the background so the eye can focus on the softly swagged window valance, the bench used as a coffee table, and a gathering of fresh blooms.

Without clutter, you can still create a nostalgic feeling of age—of your room having evolved slowly over time—by layering on a variety of wood finishes. Instead of matched suites of pieces, choose chairs, tables, and chests that feature a range of dark, medium, and natural wood stains, then dot in a painted piece or two. Here, a painted rocker plays up the room's new sage scheme, while gold-painted picture frames provide a dose of sparkling contrast.

A few simple touches can turn today's ho-hum living room into tomorrow's romantic retreat. To set the stage for your own cottage room makeover: **ROMANCE THE WINDOWS.** Replace heavy or busily patterned treatments with gauzy sheers; add filmy valances to take the hard edge off blinds or shades. **SOFTEN WITH COLOR.** Roll or sponge walls with the palest of pastel paints. Then carry out the romantic feeling with a floral or checked pastel area rug or by painting a pastel checkerboard on the floor. **REPLACE A FORMAL COFFEE TABLE** with a friendlier pine table, a worn bench, or a plush ottoman.

COTTAGE redo tips

🐚 Clear the clutter to transform your living room into a true getaway in which you can relax and listen to music, read a book, or snuggle with your favorite person without distractions.

🐚 Pull up a rocker. Even in a tight spot, you probably have space for an antique armless sewing rocker, as shown below.

RUSTIC RETREAT

Yes, you can escape to your own mountain cabin or a wooded retreat without ever leaving your living room. It's easy to do when you decorate with camp style in mind. For inspiration, think of your favorite ski lodge or, perhaps, the summer camp you loved as a kid. Then, rely on rustic furnishings, a deep-toned lodge palette, plenty of rugged texture, and a few bold geometric patterns reminiscent of Indian blankets to turn the dream into reality.

It does not matter whether this inspired camp cottage-style living area is situated on a mountainside or in the heart of the city, because this style isn't dependent on geography. What counts is its rugged look and feet-up informality. Furniture made of twigs and logs, no-nonsense outdoor-flavored stripes, and western-style motifs on toss pillows combine to create a rustic retreat. Here, the room's under-the-eaves architecture, emphasized with exposed beams, contributes to the especially cozy, cabinlike atmosphere. Outdoor gear completes the look.

DO A BACKGROUND CHECK to get going. There's nothing wrong with plain painted drywall, but don't overlook the tactile appeal created by textured plaster or painted paneling.

ADD BACK-ROADS FLAVOR with furnishings of twig, iron, or pine. Outdoor Adirondack chairs make ideal camp-style companions when moved indoors and softened with cushions. Include upholstered pieces, too. Leather is a natural, but even a twig sofa provides the necessary comfort with thick cushions.

USE RUSTIC ACCENTS. Take a sofa to camp by tossing on pillows clad in blanket-pattern fabrics. Aged sporting goods, from snowshoes to worn fishing creels, add wit to walls.

COTTAGE CUE. Having a hard time finding rugged furniture? A child's chunky, unfinished pine bed becomes a camp-style daybed when you wrap the mattress in a boldly patterned blanket or a plaid flannel sheet and pile on the bright pillows.

THE FOUR SEASONS

Navy-blue fabrics in a striking mix of cabana stripes and scenic toile cool down this home's sunny porch. The enclosed porch's wall of exterior siding remains untouched —a readymade cottage accent.

When you're putting your own cottage decorating dreams into play, it only makes sense to use your home's spaces as you see fit. Forget your rooms' labels, and recast rooms to suit your needs—and your style. If, for instance, your idea of the perfect afternoon is one spent lolling around on the porch, why not create a "porch" that you can enjoy every day—in every season? With a little wicker and some garden-fresh colors and fabrics, you can turn an enclosed porch into a year-round living area—or transform a plain-Jane living room into an airy, porch-style getaway

With wicker and paint, you can turn your living room into a year-round "porch." Here, yellow-painted walls create a sunny glow, rain or shine—and an upbeat garden theme that's enhanced by the bright quilt, fresh flowers and greenery, and a landscape print. Polished wood floors, trim blinds, and— what else?—a wicker sofa and chairs enhance the bright porch look.

If yours is an enclosed all-weather porch, enjoy the room's built-in character—plentiful windows and some interior walls that may be covered in exterior siding. If sunlight is excessive, add blinds to fend off the rays, and cover pillows and cushions in fade-resistant outdoor fabrics.

To give porch-style ambience to a living room, paint the walls a warm color, such as sun yellow or sunset peach, then add bright cotton area rugs. Consider new wicker or water hyacinth seating pieces clad in snappy stripes and fresh florals.

COTTAGE CUE. Even if your porch or sunroom was built for year-round use, add window shades to save heat and deflect the sun. Honeycomb shades, for instance, can add a measure of insulation yet tuck away beneath fabric valances.

DINING ROOMS

Dining is one of life's little pleasures —

especially when the dining room itself

serves up relaxing cottage-style

ambience. Formality fades when

furniture finishes are casual

and rooms are planned with

extra comfort, personality, and

even some fun in mind.

DOABLE DREAMS

COTTAGE
redo tip

Metal outdoor furniture makes an easy transition indoors with the help of a dainty floral print on the chairs and a fabric runner on the table. A cupboard pulled between two windows lends texture and architectural impact.

❧ Bring a fantasy garden room to fruition, and set the tone for casual dining with garden furniture. For an al fresco accent, paint an oversized clay pot, and tuck in some plants.

Decorating fantasies can be fun—but frustrating if the dreams demand more time or money than you're willing to give. Happily, there are simple, affordable methods and materials to add cottage charm and softness to your dining spot.

GET ROLLING. It's amazing what a little pastel paint can do when it's lavished on the four walls. In an afternoon, you can roll on a coat of relaxing cotton-candy colors to turn a bland dining room into one that will give your eyes a break—and your spirits a lift. And, if you think pale pink or coral walls look dreamy in daylight, wait until you see how beautifully they glow when lamps, the chandelier, and candles are all lit at night.

Blushing walls make this dining room a standout, in spite of its age and ordinary architecture. A floor-length curtain visually lengthens the short window while also adding a perky touch of color and pattern. A coat of paint and fresh fabric on the seats refreshes the chairs. Ceramic fish plates and platters hang on the wall to create a fun cottage accent, while the tabletop's pitcher of flowers makes short work of creating a centerpiece.

JAZZ UP THE CHAIRS with color. Reviving chair seats often is as simple as removing the screws that hold the seats in place, wrapping the cushions with fresh fabric, and stapling the fabric on the underside. Add toss pillows or tie-on cushions to plain wood seats, and consider repainting wood or metal chairs. If your old chairs are hopeless, buy unfinished or flea-market chairs to paint.

CHOOSE A DEGREE of "sweetness" to suit your personal style. Either take the new-found romance to the limit with a pastel area rug and curtains of pastel fabric or simple lace, or take the sweet edge off by making your floors and windows zones of neutrality.

ADD "ARCHITECTURE" with a tall cupboard. Consider a weathered find, or buy an unfinished piece to paint, sponge, or stencil.

COTTAGE CUE. How are you feeling? A little bold? Then give cottage style a contemporary twist with pastels that are clear and bright. Or, if you feel the need for a gentler, timeworn touch, choose the more muted tones of faded antique quilts or sun-bleached painted wood.

Carry Out The Casual Cottage Style

Open shelves can be the start of a charming dining room makeover. But what comes next? Adapt these quick ideas to add an extra helping of relaxation to your cottage dining spot.

■ Drape a quilt over the table for instant ease. Protect it with glass. ■ Replace a shiny crystal or glass chandelier with one that offers earthy texture or folk-art style. How about a curvy iron fixture? ■ For large gatherings, use two smaller tables instead of a longer formal one. ■ Mix, mix, mix! Take the formal edge off an existing "dining set" by adding a painted chair, a bench, or a wicker armchair. ■ Avoid high-gloss furniture; matte finishes are more casual. ■ Introduce cheery fabrics to chair seats. Toss cushions and small pillows into the seating for inviting, easy-chair style.

These bookshelves are actually the trompe l'oeil handiwork of an artist. But you can create the real thing with freestanding bookcases. White paint, from trim to curtain rod, pulls it all together.

CASUAL DISPLAYS

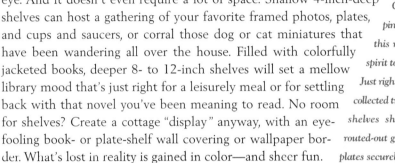

A no-fail design trick guaranteed to help your dining room strike a cute and casual pose, open display shelving also is a treat for the eye. And it doesn't even require a lot of space. Shallow 4-inch-deep shelves can host a gathering of your favorite framed photos, plates, and cups and saucers, or corral those dog or cat miniatures that have been wandering all over the house. Filled with colorfully jacketed books, deeper 8- to 12-inch shelves will set a mellow library mood that's just right for a leisurely meal or for settling back with that novel you've been meaning to read. No room for shelves? Create a cottage "display" anyway, with an eye-fooling book- or plate-shelf wall covering or wallpaper border. What's lost in reality is gained in color—and sheer fun.

Open pine shelves carry this room's cottage spirit to new heights. Just right for displaying collected treasures, such shelves should include routed-out grooves to hold plates securely in place.

ALTERNATIVE SEATING

Everybody knows that the three bears ate their porridge while sitting in chairs. But benches, love seats, and even upholstered window seats and daybeds can dish up even cozier fairy-tale cottage style for your dining room. By keeping your options open for fresh dining room seating ideas, you also can bring your rooms closer to the one-of-a-kind look so important in cottage style—much closer than marching a matched set of chairs around the table. Alternative seating breaks up the formula and drives home the cottage imperative: Create your own personal mix.

Look beyond your present dining chairs for these practical, spacemaking helpers, too:

A LONG BENCH seats three or four dinner guests in the same space as two regular chairs.

A CUSHIONED LOVE SEAT OR DAYBED can help you squeeze dining, lounging—and a lot more comfort—into the same square footage.

A BUILT-IN BANQUETTE turns a flat wall or an oddly shaped nook into an architectural asset. Hinge the top to create storage inside.

This intimate dining spot is made multipurpose, thanks to the unconventional use of a daybed to provide both seating and lounging in front of the fire. The daybed's open sides invite access from either side.

Plumped with cushions, a built-in banquette accommodates dining and lounging with equal ease in this bumped-out greenhouse space. Cottage staples, these wicker armchairs round out the grouping. Wired to a dimmer, the pendant can serve for dining or reading.

A daybed that's plumped with soft blue-and-white cushions not only enhances the Scandinavian style of this dining room, but it also gives the space a second life as a den when company leaves and the dishes are cleared away. A shapely, painted floor screen softens the corner.

BOLD STROKES

Bold color invigorates the spirit and the appetite, turning dining rooms into especially inviting places for enjoying good food—and good company. Slathering the dining room walls with eye-popping paint can create a striking cottage scheme, especially if your dream is of a sunny beach house. But what if your dreams fall on the subtler, more earthy side of cottage style? No problem. To achieve a crisp, clean look that's still lively, think of bold or brilliant colors as decorative "garnishes" to be used in small but eye-appealing doses.

LEAVE WALLS NEUTRAL and play with color the easy way using furnishings and accessories.

CREATE A COLORFUL FOCAL POINT with a boldly painted storage piece. A green, blue, or brick-red hutch or corner cupboard can play host to displays that change color with the seasons.

USE BOLDLY CONTRASTING ACCENTS in a centerpiece, toss pillows, or a table runner. If painted furniture is a cool color, complement it with warm-hued accessories—and vice versa.

PAINT THE WOODWORK a rich color to contrast with the walls and to create a little geometric drama.

Forest green chairs and trim deliver strong yet natural color to this farmhouse dining spot.

A skinny peri-winkle-blue corner cupboard consumes minimal space but conveys major color. Neutral walls and unadorned windows heighten the effect. Dinnerware and napkins add more vivid color that can easily be changed.

Introducing Bold Color

Use these pointers to choose some bold colors in your dining spot.

■ If you're going for a happy and upbeat feeling, pick warm colors—reds, yellows, or oranges. When teamed with some bright new dinnerware, a pair of painted red chairs, for instance, will reenergize any eating area. ■ To maintain a more restful mood, use serene cool colors, such as blue, green or purple, in bold ways. The blue corner piece at left is one example. ■ Mix finishes for interest. If the chairs are painted, for example, consider a natural wood table.

FRESH AIRS
— window seats

Into the Garden

Why stop at the window? If you have a porch, patio, or gazebo, take the dining experience outdoors.

Think for a moment about the kind of cottage dining spot you've always wanted or, perhaps, enjoyed at a special inn—one consisting of a charming table set in front of breezy French doors. Sound appealing? The good news is that, even if your own view is of a patio instead of an alpine lake or a suburban meadow instead of a mountain, you can enhance your daily dining experience—and your room's cottage style. Just center your table in front of your own French doors or sliders. Visual contact with the outdoors makes mealtime more interesting with the ever-changing scenery. And the outdoor view actually works like a design element, creating the natural garden look that cottage style is all about. If your view is uninspiring, relax; you can still cozy up to the glass and make the most of attractive, multipaned atrium doors. Use them as a backdrop for a charming dining spot, treating the glass to simple sheers or café-style half-curtains for a combination of cheeriness and privacy.

An ice cream table flanked by a pair of captain's chairs opens up the best view in the home to intimate dining possibilities. Salvaged door-length shutters add architectural character while providing privacy when needed.

Placing an overhead fixture near a window or glass-paned door defines that space for dining; all that's left is to move a table and chairs directly beneath it. This is an easy way to convert one end of a family room over to multipurpose use for casual dining. When the table's not used for meals, it can function as a library or game table—or just another spot to linger with friends.

■ Go for the view. Plant your table and chairs on the garden side of a porch to take in the flowers. ■ Make it private. If you can't avoid getting too near driveways, garages, and neighbors' fields of vision, screen off a dining spot with trellis panels. ■ Screen out the sun. If your outdoor dining spot is on an open deck or patio, consider adding an arbor or a retractable awning. On a covered porch, add simple canvas or matchstick roll-up shades to lower as needed. ■ Step to the side. Why not add a cafe table and chairs to a narrow side yard to create an intimate dining spot? A section of privacy fencing can host climbing ivy or potted plants in metal holders made especially for fences. ■ Take your indoor color scheme outside the easy way with toss pillows, dishes, and napkins when ready-made outdoor chair cushions don't offer your favorite colors.

FRESH AIRS
— out in the open

There's nothing new about dining outdoors, but when you have a cottage dream in your heart, be sure to put comfort, color, and even a touch of cuteness on your decorating "menu." A few easy-to-add accessories can make the most of your al fresco eating spot, enhancing the picnic appeal of a midday lunch or the unexpected romance of dinner under moonlit skies.

FIND THE RIGHT TABLE. Before choosing your outdoor table, decide how you want to use your dining space. If you typically feed a crowd, it's better to go with a picnic-size table. An unfinished pine picnic table from the home center looks great when simply varnished or brightened with a coat of white or yellow exterior enamel. If you lean toward desserts at midnight or morning coffee for two, a bistro-style table-for-two may be all you need. Even indoor tables can go outside when they're wearing two coats of exterior enamel. Whatever the table:

CHANGE THE MOOD from day to night with a pretty cloth and candle lanterns whose flames won't succumb to the inevitable gusts of wind. **ADD INDOOR STYLE** with pillows and cushions made with outdoor fabrics and moisture-resistant filling. Underfoot, go for portable, fair-weather rugs of bright cotton, sisal, or painted canvas to anchor the dining spot.

Ready any outdoor table for cottage romance by dressing it in a long fabric skirt topped with a second lace or cutwork cloth. On this screened porch, other cottage accents, from birdhouses to flowers, welcome family and guests in colorful style. With a good roof overhead, you can dress the table with fabric and lace as you would indoors. But carry toss pillows and natural fiber rugs inside when not in use to protect them from humidity and blown-in rain.

It takes only a few soft, bright touches to turn a basic porch into a colorful outdoor dining spot. An Adirondack bench and wicker chairs team with colorful cushions, whimsical pillows, and folk art to set the inviting look. Lattice panels add a bit of privacy and summery style as they filter sunlight.

SIMPLE PLEASURES

Ruffles and flourishes may be fine for folks who prefer romantic cottage rooms, but if you lean toward the more rustic side of cottage style, think simple and adopt a no-frills approach. Plain, honest fare that relies on natural textures and materials will create just the right warm, easygoing setting for gathering around your table. **START WITH THE FURNITURE.** A scrubbed or distressed natural wood, such as pine or oak, is your best bet for suggesting rusticity. Primitive styling figures in, too: Keep table and chair shapes basic, and avoid shiny finishes, carving, and intricately turned legs or spindles. **SOFTEN A RUSTIC TABLE** with textiles—tablecloths, runners, placemats, and napkins—and, of course, bouquets of fresh flowers gathered in primitive jars or a watering can. **EXPRESS YOUR INTERESTS.** Plain style lends itself as readily to whimsical contemporary artwork as to primitive birdhouses or redware, so opt for accessories that you truly love. **LET WALLS SPEAK PLAINLY** and stand on their own without pattern. The best guideline is simplicity—no papers, patterns, or decorative paints.

Rustic translates as honest simplicity in this dining room where the texture and patina of wood supply the warmth. Leaving the chairs uncushioned and the table uncovered, except for a rag runner, enhances the primitive mood. The wood-clad walls—natural, with traces of a rubbed-off green stain—get all the adornment they need from a tall cupboard and its homey display of dishes and books.

Mismatched country chairs, a basic farm table, and a painted cupboard create a plain but pretty background for contemporary art, stylish tableware, and a few whimsical accessories.

COTTAGE CUE. Create a rustic look through simplicity: Leave walls and windows uncovered. Then cut the rough edges with a movable feast of decorative accents on the table—especially linens and flowers.

A CLEAN CANVAS

Because it is naturally light and airy, a dining room with a wall or two of windows makes a natural canvas on which you can create your own cottage style. By lightening the backgrounds, you can make the most of such a light-filled space—or even create an illusion of light to open up a room that's not quite as well endowed with windows.

DO IT WHITE. Paint walls, ceilings, trim, and built-ins white to let natural light play out its own artistry and create a fresh glow.

VARY THE SHADES of white. For interest, use one white for the ceilings, another for walls, and still another for wood trimwork, varying from crisp cool whites to warmer tones.

OPEN THE DOORS. Once the backgrounds are rendered crisp, enhance airiness by leaving windows and glass doors uncovered. If your dining spot includes built-in cupboards, remove some of their doors—or replace a section of solid doors with sparkling glass.

AVOID A STERILE LOOK by adding a bit of pattern and color with textiles on the table and chairs.

PLAN FOR EVENINGS when a white-on-white room can wear a little thin. Work in lots of creamy yellow lamplight, and consider white window shades to lower when darkness arrives.

Strands of English ivy trained along the windows in this solarium dining space add the interest of a window treatment without blocking the views or cluttering the clean white backgrounds. The ivy's green hue is repeated in minimal fashion by thin green moldings that run both horizontally and vertically like a picture frame around the room. An old-fashioned white cloth with blue checks lightens the look of the natural wood table; white-painted chairs add light, too, emphasizing the jolt of color on the armchair.

A white background creates a spacious look in this snug breakfast nook—an illusion enhanced by glass doors and a sliver of mirror below the cabinets. The built-in banquette creates space-efficient seating beneath the window.

CREATING COTTAGE STYLE

BEDROOMS

Cottage is a "one-size-fits-all" style, working its magic in bedrooms of virtually any size or shape. Ranging from rustic to refined, cottage furnishings, colors, and accents can play up the inherent coziness of a small sleep spot or turn an oversized bedroom into a wonderfully snug retreat.

The Art of Composing

To create eye-catching arrangements of your favorite things, keep these pointers in mind.

■ Include the wall when making arrangements on a tabletop or a night stand. Hung low on the wall above a nightstand and lamp, for example, a framed print or a favorite plate or straw hat adds personality as it draws the eye upward. ■ Let varied textures play together. Slick porcelain, rough wicker, shiny glass, and weathered wood enjoy each other's company. ■ For a casual look, keep informal balance in mind and build a grouping around one larger, asymmetrically placed object. Above a bed or chest, for instance, balance an off-center painting with two small plates or prints. ■ For more formality, set identical objects symmetrically on each side of an imaginary line down a grouping's center.

GETTING IN THE MOOD

It's true; little things *do* mean a lot, especially when it comes to setting the mood in cottage bedrooms. Personal and intimate, sleeping places gain much of their cozy charm from decorative accents that reflect who you are and what you love. Such accessories also work their decorating magic as vehicles that transport your eye and psyche to the cottage getaway of your dreams. Here's how:

START SMALL. Instead of embarking on major redecorating, strip your room to its basic furniture pieces; chances are that a few finishing touches can give cottage style to many of your major furnishings.

REWORK THE BASICS. Feeling romantic? Replace a hard-edged nightstand with a skirted table or a burlap lampshade with a silky one. Yearn for a frontier cabin? Bring in a rough pine or twig nightstand or desk, or place a weathered bench at the foot of your bed.

LET DETAILS COUNT. Even functional items, from lotion bottles to clocks, have a cottage decorating role to play. All-important personal photos also foster your style when their frames, whether of fine silver or rough pine, are in sync with your cottage vision.

Little things add up to big style in this bedroom corner. A quaint writing table takes the place of an ordinary nightstand. The vintage portrait and dog figurines impart a nostalgic feeling that's echoed by small but meaningful touches that include the flowery rug and a painted wastebasket.

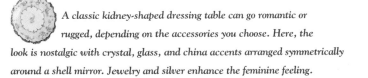

A classic kidney-shaped dressing table can go romantic or rugged, depending on the accessories you choose. Here, the look is nostalgic with crystal, glass, and china accents arranged symmetrically around a shell mirror. Jewelry and silver enhance the feminine feeling.

COMFORTS OF A B&B

"Simplify, simplify" to keep a bedroom from becoming busy. Choose a bed with simple flowing lines, and pare other pieces to an essential few. Then use spirited yet easy-on-the-eye colors. Here, a high-contrast, complementary scheme of pastel yellow and lavender is soothing yet lively.

The bath may be new, but antique fixtures make it look as if it's always been there. A new step-up platform subtly separates the bath from the sleeping area—and creates space to run plumbing lines. Matching the bed skirt, the curtain softens the bath and adds a hint of privacy.

Why not visit a country bed-and-breakfast inn—whenever you like and without leaving home? You can if you do a makeover with cottage style in mind. Here's how to create suite comforts without adding on an inch.

BATHE YOURSELF IN STYLE. Turn the end of a bedroom into a bath. The trick: A raised platform eases the installation of plumbing lines. Time spent scouting for old fixtures pays charming dividends with a footed tub and a pedestal sink. In a tight spot, use a curtain at one side and a low wall at the other for a sense of privacy without claustrophobia.

FIND A CHARMING NEW BED. Painted white, a curvy new wood or iron bed will set the romantic rural mood and fit modern-day bedding.

PILE ON THE COMFORT with a fat comforter and a featherbed. (New featherbeds slide into their own washable cases and plop right over a mattress.) An antique quilt can delight the eye and inspire a cottage color scheme carried out with wallpaper and a painted or tiled floor.

COTTAGE
redo tip

🐦 A wide Shaker-style peg railing adds architectural interest to plain walls. Higher than a chair rail and lower than a plate rail, it creates hanging and display space in rooms where every inch truly counts.

Breaking Out Of The Suburban Box

When a small bedroom feels merely claustrophobic— instead of cottage cozy—it's time for a few decorative tricks to open things up.

■Paint walls, window trim, and doors white for a smooth flow of space. ■ Give newfound depth and dimension to flat walls. Add a chair rail a third of the way up from the floor or a plate rail about 18 inches down from the ceiling. For cottage charm, add white paneling below either rail. ■Angle a furniture piece. Set an armoire or a chair across a corner. Or, angle the bed and nestle it against a corner-spanning shelf or storage unit. ■Open up by hanging a large mirror behind the bed, above a desk, or anywhere you want to "punch a hole" in a wall. Just be sure the mirror reflects something that you want to see, such as a window across the room.■Opt for charming but light accessories, such as the aged shutters, white pitcher, and see-through birdcage at right.

COTTAGE IN THE 'BURBS

— summer romance

Turn your bedroom into a breezy seaside retreat and coax it out of its modern box at the same time. Lots of white and a few fool-the-eye tricks are quick tickets to paradise.

TRY A NEW ANGLE. An angled bed takes up a bit more square footage, but it makes up for the loss by expanding visual space with its room-widening diagonal line. Here, the bed's placement also turns the two separate windows into one bolder unit. A custom triangular cabinet also pulls things together while efficiently handling display and storage duties.

ADD ARCHITECTURAL OOMPH. Make windows appear wider with louvered wooden shutters that open flat against the walls. Painted white, stock shutters also add a breezy, seashore look to any room. Moldings and white paneling add character, too.

BLOW THE LID OFF THE PLACE with a sky-and-cloud treatment. Paint the ceilings with pale blue latex paint, let dry, and then sponge on a few clouds. Or, copy the treatment shown here, and simply hang a cloud-patterned wallpaper above white paneling that stops short of the ceiling line. Now, toss on some celestial blue bed linens, and lie back to watch the clouds drift by.

White-painted wood, whether in the form of sheets of paneling or in planks of wood, combines the texture and breeziness of a beach house with just enough depth to display starfish. Sea urchins, shells, and small salvaged shutters on the built-in headboard also suggest a seaside cottage feeling that's reinforced by the windows' white louvered shutters.

COTTAGE CUE. Clouds aren't just for children's rooms. They make dreamy cottage-style motifs for adults, too. Use cloud-patterned wallpaper, or spray-paint or sponge your own clouds over pale blue.

COTTAGE IN THE 'BURBS
— winter cabin

OK, you guessed it; this bedroom has never been anywhere near the boondocks. Yet it provides plenty of rustic touches to transport its owners to their dreamed-of cabin—*every* night. Love the look? It's surprising how little it actually takes to get you from suburbia to this kind of rustic cottage. Here's the "map":

GET GOING with a rugged, large-scale furniture piece that will set the mood while also standing out in sharp contrast to the smooth walls. Your starting point might be a chunky log bed or a massive armoire with a natural or weathered finish.

MOVE ON to smaller pieces with texture—a twig table, a bench, baskets, and a rough-hewn chair and table.

TURN UP THE HEAT. Think of an old iron stove as an artful accessory to repaint and put on display. Or, lean a salvaged fireplace surround against the wall.

ADD PLANTS and flowers to suggest mountain meadows.

SNUGGLE IN. Floral and plaid fabric patterns in rich colors are full-bodied enough to go equal partners with the rustic furniture when the designs are large in scale.

Featuring the natural shapes of trees just chopped down in the woods, this bed is the focal point that provides rustic camp character to a suburban bedroom. Instead of Native American or cowboy motifs, the fabrics here are less expected. Florals, stripes, and plaids are bold enough in color and scale to hold their own against weighty furniture pieces.

Yes, you really can create this cabin fantasy in a flash— even if your present "hideout" is a suburban condo bedroom like this. The old stove and stove pipe are just-for-looks treasures painted and propped up for instant warmth. The antique chair and worn table help foster the rustic illusion, as does the woven rug.

COTTAGE FOR KIDS

Let your own budding cottage style burst into full bloom in your child's rooms. This is the place in which you can comfort your kid while also giving your own cottage fantasies free rein. Here are tips to get you going.

THINK SMALL. Let wee ones live happily ever after with child-size versions of furniture made for big people. Iron beds with whimsical cottage-creature finials, wicker chairs, and painted chests can last through youth and become tomorrow's heirlooms.

PLAY DRESS UP. Accent hand-me-down furniture with new paint and hardware.

PERSONALIZE. Embellish with one-of-a-kind touches—heirloom baby clothes from both sides of the family, quilts, old toys, collections (it's never too early to start!), and art. Decorate with museum prints of children. Or, disassemble a children's book, and frame the illustrations. Even an array of colorful china on the walls will stimulate your child's eye and brain—and serve as a cottage counterpoint to plastic toys. Or hang a charming cottage wallpaper border at kiddie eye level.

Storytime is what this well-dressed child's bed is all about, with its rabbit finials sitting sentinel on the bedposts. Set for tea and paired with wicker chairs, a painted table inspires hours of "make believe." Vintage clothing and hats on a Shaker peg rack contribute to the one-of-a-kind style.

Secondhand cribs may be tempting, but for safety's sake, look for new cribs with antique styling—beds that meet modern safety standards with slats no more than 2 ⅜ inches apart and, of course, no lead paint.

COTTAGE CUE. Choose window and wall treatments that are age neutral (such as striped or checked wallpaper or fabrics) to create a nursery that can easily grow up as your child does.

BATHROOMS

It takes so little to give cottage charm to a basic bath. Sometimes, the transforming ingredient is nothing more than a touch of cheery fabric skirting a dated sink, a fresh frill at the window, or a bold color rolled onto a wall. As you'll see in this chapter, even the choice and arrangement of toiletries and decorative accents on a small shelf can make a personal difference.

SEAFARING STYLE

Keep beach-house hopes alive with exuberantly overscaled waves painted to form a watery frieze. The round mirrors—think of them as portholes—and, of course, a snappy toy sailboat carry on the fun. To make waves, cut your own stencil from acetate.

Whether inspired by Key West or the Caribbean, this bright bath gets its away-from-it-all ambience from witty waves and tile-style checks painted in tropical colors.

What better place to play out fantasies of a waterfront cottage than in the bath? Even if your home is hopelessly landlocked, your bath can sweep you away on waves of seacoast colors or on the decks of teeny boats. Start with ocean blue or coral pink paints, fish or wave motifs, cabana stripes, seashells—and even a kiddie sand bucket to hold soaps and sponges—to capture the spirit. Next, use these less obvious ways to get the rest of your senses in a getaway mood.

NOW HEAR THIS. Tune out workaday noises of traffic or the kids' TV and get your psyche in a seafaring mood with the sound of waves. Plug in a wave machine that sends the relaxing rhythm of the surf through the room, or use an audio tape or CD with sounds of the real thing. Now, close your eyes and let your mind sail off to a more serene place.

TAKE A DIP. Make the most of the water you *do* have. A shower is fine in the mornings, but why not take time to indulge in a long, rejuvenating splash in the tub at night?

A few accessories put getaway character into a basic bath. Here, the owner let a touch of the sea roll in by displaying sailboat models and adding a compass design to the floor. Love the idea? Paint a simpler compass design onto a round of primed canvas, then protect with polyurethane.

PAINT A MOOD

This painted mural brings more than a romantic landscape to this bath. It refreshes and relaxes with greens and blues balanced by warm tones to keep the energy level up. For a scenic bath, hire a local artist or look for wall covering murals that replicate rural scenes.

Take a modern tub back in time with a frame clad in white wood paneling. Here, the subtlety of the white-painted wood teams with a worn chair to add character—and changing colors is as easy as putting out a stack of fresh towels.

This is a test: Which of the baths on these two pages reaches out to grab your eye—and your heart? Which one would you rather wake up to in the morning? It's no secret that colorful paint is a magic potion that can change a room's mood. But how do you decide on your own scheme? Go with your gut.

ENERGIZE. If the yellow bath makes your heart sing, you like stimulation. Roll on yellow or orange for cheeriness—or red to really fire up your passions.

RELAX. If the soft-toned baths get your attention, you're looking for some down time. Calm yourself by painting on some cool colors. Green and blue will refresh you; blue and purple produce the most tranquil feelings.

HAVE IT ALL. Unsure about your color choices? No problem. Plan on white walls and a wardrobe of colorful towels that will let you change the room's mood on a whim.

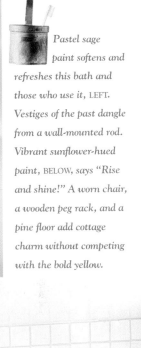

Pastel sage paint softens and refreshes this bath and those who use it, LEFT. Vestiges of the past dangle from a wall-mounted rod. Vibrant sunflower-hued paint, BELOW, says "Rise and shine!" A worn chair, a wooden peg rack, and a pine floor add cottage charm without competing with the bold yellow.

QUAINT CONCEPTS

The cottage-lover's quest for rooms rich with the patina of time gives you license to relax and do the very simplest of bathroom makeovers. As you contemplate redoing your bath, take a moment to look for its saving graces—remnants of the past that can anchor a new scheme with vintage charm. The plan is simple: Leave functional old fixtures and windows in place and stage a spirited revival with fresh flourishes of fabric, wall coverings, and accessories.

RESPECT THE ELDERS. Look at any decades-old sinks, tubs, and tile with a fresh eye. If they say "cottage," they may be fine as is—or may be candidates for a fresh finish. Epoxy paints can work wonders but are best left in the hands of professional refinishers.

FAKE THE ARCHITECTURE of the past. Forego the urge to make things sleek and glossy, and repeat the lines and textures of yesteryear with wood. Nail up crown molding at the ceiling line, or cover the lower third of the wall with that beloved cottage staple—white beaded-board paneling.

BUILD COTTAGE CHARACTER with almost grandmotherly simplicity, using pure white towels and soaps and demure lace or cotton window valances to crown billowing curtains or half-curtains.

What a shame it would have been to hide this window with a modern shower. The homeowner smartly chose to keep the freestanding tub—and the cottage charm that it imparts. A sheer tapered valance adds the lovable look of grandma's house.

What's wrong with being old, anyway? Instead of hiding its age, this bath proudly shows it off with coats of paint that add fresh colors without covering its antique farmhouse appearance. A few plants and towels make short work of accessorizing.

This wall-hung sink and old tub were functional catalysts for a decorative change that nods to the past. Checked fabric takes the frilly forms of a balloon shade on the window and a gathered skirt on the sink to soften hard edges.

COTTAGE redo tips

❧ Don't let an old floor covering lower your spirits. For a quick fix, cover as much as you can with a colorful woven rug. If the floor is beyond salvaging, start over with a checkerboard of vinyl tiles, the plainest sheet vinyl you can find, or pine-look laminate flooring. Ceramic tiles are beautiful but may require a new subfloor.

NATURE'S STAMPS

If you long for a peaceful decorating scheme with just a touch of subtle pattern, Mother Nature whispers a response. The great outdoors is an abundant repository of delightful designs perfect for the cottage-style bath. When painted in pale colors, a scattering of leaves, flowers, or fern fronds can carry a theme without overwhelming even the smallest bath—or the most harried brain. Scatter leaves across a wall, or use them as a border for a shower curtain, towel, or rug.

PICK A MOTIF. Use your own or ready-made stamps and stencils.

MAKE STAMPS. To make your own leaf stamps, choose two or three supple leaves from the yard, or buy preserved leaves at a crafts stores. Trace each leaf onto foam-core board; cut out each outline with a crafts knife. Use double-stick tape to affix each real leaf to its foam-core shape, leaving the sides with the most pronounced veins exposed.

STAMP AND BRUSH. Brush or roll acrylic paint onto the leaf; gently press onto the wall or fabric; let dry. Brush on pastel pink paint to fill in any gaps in the leaf patterns.

A flat-weave area rug makes a good canvas for painted-on designs. Stamped leaves along the end of this rug offer convincing testimony to the beauty of moderation: Its limited appearance and subtle palette increases the pattern's impact.

Flat linen towels possess natural charm, thanks to a gathering of stamped-on leaves. With its light finish and exposed knots, the pine shelf makes its own respectful nod to nature.

The handpainted motif running throughout this small bath gives it one-of-a-kind character while preserving its inherent cottage simplicity. Leaf patterns are stamped across the borders of the shower curtain and again along the chair rail on the wall.

KITCHENS

Cottage design is made to order for folks who see the kitchen as the hub of the home. As you'll discover while turning these pages, the cottage kitchen staples are simple, basic—and utterly charming. Although they speak softly, they do, indeed, have major impact when it comes to transforming even a bland kitchen into an inviting gather-round space.

COTTAGE STAPLES

Whether you're considering a new kitchen or spicing up an old one, stock your pantry of decorating ideas with these cottage staples. The recipe, of course, is your own, so use as many of these ingredients as you see fit.

CHEERY COLOR. Country mornings are at hand when you work warm colors into your plan using tile, paint, or textiles.

WHITE PLUS WOOD. White adds freshness, purity, and airiness; a touch of pine (even if only on stools, picture frames, and woody baskets) brings warmth.

OPEN DISPLAY. Replace a section of solid cabinet doors with glass doors, a plate rack, or open bookshelves.

FOLKISH ACCENTS. Love birdhouses, metal sculpture, or hand-painted china or boxes? Use them to bring fresh personality.

WHITE CURTAINS. Half-curtains work especially well if your view is a city street or a neighbor's home.

COMFORT. Tuck a wicker armchair into a corner. Or if you *really* eat at the counter, turn a dining nook into a sitting spot with a love seat. An existing hutch can display colorful, mood-setting collectibles.

HOMEY SURPRISES. Look beyond the kitchen for accents. Why *not* let a candlestick lamp accent a backsplash?

Furnishings, including an antique pine stepback cupboard, a love seat, and a coffee table, transform this nook into an inviting family gathering spot. Simple half-curtains add day-long privacy and softness, too.

Open up! Replacing sections of closed cabinets with a plate rack and cookbook shelves pays practical and decorative dividends. These easily accessible shelves keep plates handy. For visible but closed storage, have cabinet doors replaced with glass fronts. Decoratively framed mirrors open up the walls and doors.

This kitchen has all the elements you need to cook up some cheery cottage style. In addition to the decorating staples listed above, take a cue from the table in the foreground and gather your own blooms in anything from mason jars to jelly glasses, all set atop a cutwork cloth.

COTTAGE FACELIFTS

Little turns into larger than life with a few cottage quick fixes. Cabinets replaced with open shelves and umber-washed walls open up the kitchen with a Tuscan flair.

Let an aging kitchen speak about the past. Simply paint cabinets, accenting old half-round shelves with paint. Blue-and-white accents boldly contrast yellow walls. Personalize with funky touches, such as this clock collection and the license plate on a drawer front.

Wake up a dull brown kitchen with fresh green and white tile, checkered pantry doors, glass insets for cabinet doors, and a backsplash shelf. An old fridge gains new charm when the front is covered with a chalkboard held in place with construction adhesive.

Solve kitchen challenges with strategies garnered from these three creative kitchens redesigns. **LEAVE WELL ENOUGH ALONE.** Start a quick and budget-conscious facelift by recognizing and keeping the gems of the past. An old tiled backsplash or a tiled countertop may be fine as is—or a candidate for a quick revival with colored grout. Fresh paint and drawer pulls revive cabinets. Cottage accents, from wall-hung plates to open spice shelves, finish the job. **BUILD CHARACTER** in a new kitchen with shelves that turn plain walls into display spots. For some fresh color and texture, sponge walls or antique cabinets. **BRING ON THE FUNK.** Mix collectible old fans and appliances, such as toasters, with anything from bright Fiestaware to antique teacups to create your own look.

COTTAGE redo tip

Want to paint old cabinets? For the neatest job, remove the doors and hardware and take out the drawers. Work on a flat surface. For stained finishes, remove the gloss by sanding or applying liquid sandpaper. Use a deglossing agent before painting. When painting or staining, work with, not against, the wood grain.

OPEN DISPLAYS

Modern kitchens, for all their buttoned-up cabinetry and sleek surfaces, take to cottage style with ease. Countertops, for example, needn't be swept free of everyday utensils after each meal. A favorite cookie jar and a colander full of fresh fruit on permanent countertop display is a first step from utilitarian chill to homey personality. If space allows, keep a pretty teapot and teacups arranged on a tray and ready for guests.

RETHINK YOUR CABINETS when you're ready to venture farther into a cottage conversion for your kitchen. Install a new, ready-made plate rack in place of an existing cabinet section, or remove a single upper cabinet door to put the charm of cookbooks and collections in full view. To display glass and china while keeping dust at bay, replace one section of upper cabinet doors with new glass ones, or have a carpenter remake existing doors, replacing panels of wood with glass.

LOOK FOR OPEN WALL SPACE that's big enough for a spice rack, a plate rack, a pot rack, or display shelves. Turn the window into a garden spot by spanning it with glass shelves and adding a lineup of growing herbs or flowers. Use wall space behind an older stove, too, for a practical place to show off handsome but functional cooking tools on hooks or on a wire grid.

ADD A BAKER'S RACK to turn a leftover wall space or corner into a tall focal point. Available in a variety of sizes, the racks can hold plants, accessories, and cookbooks. Save drawer space by gathering odds and ends in baskets on rack shelves.

As a quick redo, remove the door of a cabinet next to a window, and add a strip of decorative molding at the top to introduce a standard kitchen to cottage style. A brass plate rail along the top shelf and dowel rods as the bottom-shelf plate rack complete the look. Colorful pottery can add garden-style finishing touches.

Neatly arranged and close at hand, much-used kitchen tools take full advantage of the wall space behind the stove. Matching red handles contribute to the casual decor, as do the pottery bowls on the decorative shelf above. Use glass jars in interesting shapes to store staples within easy reach, and organize wooden spoons and other cooking necessities in a colorful container.

This kitchen speaks well of cottage style thanks to its eloquent use of wall space. A blank span of wall provides the perfect spot for a curvy-edged decorative shelf unit, a space just right for caddying coffee cups and other eye-pleasing accessories, decorative or functional.

INSTANT WAKE-UPS

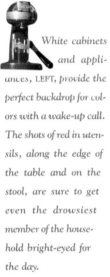

Search flea markets and thrift stores for accessories, such as the matted and framed still life and bright 1950s table-cloth, ABOVE RIGHT. *Colorful pitchers make ideal containers for casual flowers. Home-canned produce adds a heartfelt touch.*

White cabinets and appliances, LEFT, *provide the perfect backdrop for colors with a wake-up call. The shots of red in utensils, along the edge of the table and on the stool, are sure to get even the drowsiest member of the household bright-eyed for the day.*

Cobalt blue bottles serving as bud vases team with a lively folk art print to add cheery cottage color and style to a once-drab windowless sink area.

A burst or two of vibrant color is almost a must for the cottage kitchen. Perhaps because it's the room where we start the day, the need to inject a caffeinelike snap into the kitchen's decor is almost universal. Sure, you can work wonders by painting the walls or installing a colorful new floor, but perhaps all you really need is a smattering of colorful accessories. Cottage style's emphasis on collections allows you to revive any kitchen—almost instantly—with vivid color. **LEAVE THE BACKGROUNDS ALONE.** Soothing, pale neutrals will blend with the other areas of the house if you don't want to break up the flow. Have fun searching out the best and the brightest functional and decorative items to scatter around the kitchen, then trust your personal color barometer to tell you when the color level is just right. **EMPLOY SHORT-TERM COLOR.** Bright table linens allow you to change the palette every time you set the table. To raise the color level, make a more permanent statement with framed prints, a bright wall covering, or new fabric for chair or stool seats. For an earthy touch, how about the rich jewel tones of homemade jams and jellies in jars lined up along a shelf? Or recycled mayonnaise jars filled with cinnamon sticks or colorful pasta?

New cottage-style wallpaper joins original ceramic wall tiles and a jazzy pitcher to set this kitchen in colorful motion. The tabletop festivities continue with a collectible toaster, a bright vintage tablecloth, old salt and pepper shakers, and red-and-white napkins.

POTTED PLEASURES

If you love gardening or just enjoy the breezy outdoor style, here's how to playfully blur the line between your kitchen and the outdoors.

MOVE NATURE INDOORS. Outdoor furnishings of curlicued cast-iron or cast-aluminum bring parklike romance to the kitchen. Or how about rugged cedar or redwood dining pieces for a camp-style dining spot? A pine picnic table and benches can replace a boring table and chairs with images of summer at the lake. Weave some natural cottage style into your kitchen by snipping grapevines at the end of the season and twining them over windows or training vines (growing from a countertop pot) around a window frame.

GIVE YOURSELF AN EARFUL. If your growing season is short and winter days seem long, bring nature's sounds inside, too. Just as audio tapes of waves can soothe a bedroom or bath, tapes of singing birds can lift spirits and foster a garden mood in the kitchen.

TURN A WINDOW INTO A GARDEN. Create cottage gardens of herbs and other potted plants on glass shelves. (Hint: Have a brown thumb? Anyone can grow parsley on a sill!) "Plant" window sills with small clay pots, or hang larger pots in front of the windows.

In this small kitchen, cooking, clean-up, and plant spaces are combined in one corner, thanks to a low primitive bench and good use of both the window and the below-sink areas.

Even while in use, the cottage kitchen can be a joy to behold. Here the flower arrangement in progress adds to rather than detracts from the room's beauty.

A Kitchen Potting Area

Live out a garden fantasy right in your kitchen. With a few touches, it can double as that potting shed you've always wanted.

■ Use a standard-size kitchen utensil drawer to stash your gardening tools. ■ Reassign a deep pan drawer for potting soils or fertilizers. Add a silver lining with foil or protect by placing garden materials in a heavy plastic bag. ■ Bring garden tools out of the closet. Install painted Peg-Board or pine paneling, then add hooks or even plain nails for hanging trowels and trimmers. ■ Put terra cotta pots on a shelf or counter to hold garden gear and kitchen wares.

An extra sink, here installed before an oversize window, makes an idea place for the avid gardener's indoor potting bench.

This cottage kitchen design takes advantage of the big windows that already blur the distinction between indoors and out. The windows are left uncovered, and the countertops are scattered with generous bouquets of flowers and a topiary.

IN A PINCH

Think of small kitchen eating areas as cottage assets—especially cozy retreats that encourage conversation and relaxation. Often, it's these tiniest of tables and chairs that become the most popular seats in the house. With the right dining pieces, you can create an extra surface for preparing meals, places for family members or guests to sit and keep the cook company, and a quiet spot for intimate meals or some solo letter writing. A small table and two chairs or even a slim worktable with two stools tucked beneath it may be all you need.

PICK A TABLE to suit your space. When every inch counts, choose a narrow drop-leaf-style table that rests against the wall. When the sides are lifted, it converts into a functional dining surface. If you have a bit more space, fit in a small writing table or a farm table; such tables often have drawers that add needed storage for table linens.

USE SLIM CHAIRS, such as metal bistro-style or wood-slatted park chairs, that fold when not in use.

MIX SEATING for a playful cottage touch. Replace two chairs with a space-saving bench. You can mix chair styles, too, as long as they share the same scale and degree of formality. For example, country-style Windsor and ladderback chairs enjoy each other's company.

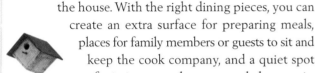

Having an enjoyable eat-in kitchen doesn't mean you have to allow enough room to feed the troops. A table for two offers ample rewards. This kitchen dining area brings life to a dull corner. The small rectangular table fits snugly against the wall and pairs with two similarly small-scaled chairs, which can be folded and stored to free up space when needed. The table can be pulled out and an extra chair or two added when more seating is needed for larger kitchen gatherings.

A new freestanding banquette makes efficient use of a sunny kitchen corner. Shelves above the windows not only carry the lines of the booth and create display space but include pegs for hanging cottage curtains.

Scour flea markets and garage sales for an old work table or even a desk that's just big enough to seat two. This room's available wall space is longer than it is deep, so the table is turned for the most efficient fit.

PORCHES

No cottage should be without an inviting fresh-air sitting spot. A classic front porch, complete with white rockers and railings, first comes to mind. But, as you'll see, cottage style allows you to create a setting that's as romantic—or as rugged—as you like. In fact, your own "porch" can even be a simple patch of lawn.

QUICK REFRESHERS

With one foot indoors and the other out, three-season porches are, indeed, fair-weather friends. It's true that they go away as soon as winter's chill arrives, but that doesn't mean they should receive less than their decorative due the rest of the year. In fact, can you think of a better place to make your getaway dreams materialize? Here are some fast ways to help any porch put on a cottage face.

TOSS ON THE COLOR. Think of ready-made pillows, rugs, and tablecloths as "makeup" to give a blush of color to a bland porch. First decide on your cottage look, then buy patterned fabrics that are *flowered* for romance, *checked* for camp style, or *striped* for a look that's just beachy.

FRESHEN WITH PAINT. Paint an old porch swing or chair picket-fence white. Also consider painting the porch floor. You can't go wrong with an all-over checkerboard design. Or, roll a light solid color over the floor, then brush on simple striped or checked area rugs to define dining and sitting areas.

Zone a porch for sitting and dining, then pile on cushions for comfort. Rocks and branches found on hikes blur the bounds between indoor and out, as does the painted floor. (To paint bare concrete, use an alkyd primer, then top with either latex or alkyd paint in either a gloss or semi-gloss finish.)

Even a quick after-work meal can feel like a mini vacation when you gather on the porch. A splashy gingham tablecloth joyously shouts "Picnic!" while the screening keeps bugs at bay. Candles and a rustic camping lantern throw a little light on the table in the evening.

With a good roof overhead, a porch can host gatherings of colorful, mood-setting accessories. Fuss-free glass and pottery join framed prints that move inside when the evening or weekend is over or storms threaten. Paint brightens the brickwork.

FULL-TIME FUNCTION

Lounge chairs with scooped seats and tilted backs gather for dining or relaxing. A wicker armchair can pull up to the table as needed or drop back and join an ottoman for lounging.

Heaped with pillows, this porch sofa, accommodates an afternoon napper or a full contingent of diners with equal ease. Matchstick blinds not only bring mottled, woody color and texture to the windows, but they also help screen out the glare.

Even enclosed porches too often end up as part-time rooms where people stop only briefly before moving into or out of the house. But why let such a precious space deteriorate into one that you just walk on by? Given the same decorative TLC that you use in other rooms, a year-round porch may, indeed, become your favorite all-weather getaway. Just raise its comfort quotient.

REPLACE worn-out furniture pieces that sway or sag with sturdier, more reassuring designs, and trade prim straight-back chairs for those that invite lingering.

COMFORT YOUR BODY. Use lounge chairs in place of the usual dining chairs. They can still gather round the dining table but also serve for reading and relaxing, especially if you provide an ottoman or two. Add laid-back comfort with a sofa—or an outdoor chaise that combines porch style with year-round pampering.

CUT THE GLARE. The sun dips lower in the sky in winter, creating the potential for more glare on year-round porches. Combat it with blinds or insulating honeycomb shades.

LIGHTEN UP. A candle chandelier works for dining, but you'll need lamps for reading. If your porch lacks electrical outlets, have new ones installed; you'll need floor plugs if your walls are floor-to-ceiling glass.

Softening the Edges for Hours of Ease

To add gentility to even the most rustic porch, borrow some of the same ideas that you use to cozy up your interior spaces. In other words, make things comfy and colorful.

■ Cover wood or metal chairs, settees, swings, and benches with pillows for pretty pattern and a softening touch. Make your own, or check out the colorful ready-made chair and settee cushions at import and discount stores. ■ For comfort's sake, add cushions to seats and chair backs, too. Or, drape a fuzzy throw or padded quilt across a chair back for physical comfort and visual delight. ■ Keep your porch's rustic floor and walls in check with generous amounts of fabric over furnishings. ■ At the dining table, pile on layers with multiple table skirts and linen place mats and napkins. ■ Soften small endtables with fabric, too; even a cloth napkin can make a stylish difference.

SUMMER-CAMP STYLE

Taking your personal style outside to your porch or yard is one of the best ways to turn your home into a well-rounded retreat that immerses you and your psyche in the cottage of your dreams. Before you choose your porch furnishings, take a moment to let your mind wander—again—to the kind of getaway you've always wanted. Are images of favorite vacations at rustic lodges or summer camps in the Ozarks, Adirondacks, or Rockies calling you? Is your cottage ideal a little house in the big woods? Then let rugged furnishings take you there. Enhance the rough-and-tumble look with bold hues and few fabrics, patterns, or decorative details to smooth the rough edges. The goal is to emulate the outdoors, not tame it. Go heavy with the textures of twigs and bark. Include wicker, iron, and cane. A few decorative outdoor pieces, such as birdhouses and weather vanes, carry the theme.

Simplicity and a dark, polished palette are the keys to this porch's handsome good looks. By suggesting long, languid summer afternoons, the gathering of easygoing rockers makes even a few after-work moments especially relaxing. Much of the space's charm and ease comes from what's missing: busy patterns and fabrics.

Even if they're just for looks, added-on tree-trunk posts give woodsy style to a porch. Rough-hewn log furniture, mini birdhouse cabins, and bright lodge colors and patterns (in blanket-style throws and a rug) convey camp style.

POTTING-SHED AMBIENCE

If you can't pass a plant without checking to see how it's doing—if you tend to lose yourself in pinching, potting, and watering—then consider a porch that speaks to that side of your cottage character. Not only is a garden potting shed scheme relaxing for humans, but it can make your leafy friends happy, too. After all, it *isn't* easy being green these days, and your plants will appreciate the chance to spend more time in your loving care. To turn your porch into a garden "shed" with all the comforts of loam, consider these simple tips.

COVER WALLS with rough wood planks to suggest the inside of a decades-old garden structure. Stain planks or paint them white depending on your taste and the amount of light the porch enjoys. **ADD A POTTING BENCH.** A home center workbench kit makes a flexible surface for potting plants or serving casual drinks. **BRING THE GARDEN IN** with plants and flowery pillows. **FILTER LIGHT** with shades that don't completely block the view.

The corner just behind the settee could be just another dull spot. The clever home-owner turned it into a garden accent with a birdhouse, plant, art piece, and a stack of books rising up from a hidden table. Plants, potting tools, and a squash-look teapot add garden romance around the room.

Create a potting-shed-style focal point with an old worktable or a new workbench. Witty birdhouses on poles (or garden gear on shelves) add needed height. A varnished work surface can serve for potting or, when scrubbed, for hosting casual buffets or after-dinner drinks.

ON THE FARM

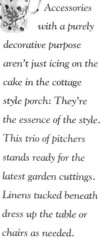

Accessories with a purely decorative purpose aren't just icing on the cake in the cottage style porch: They're the essence of the style. This trio of pitchers stands ready for the latest garden cuttings. Linens tucked beneath dress up the table or chairs as needed.

Whether in reality or in the mind's eye, the postcard-pretty porches of America's classic farmhouses still beckon. If your cottage ideal takes you down gravel roads or country lanes to a mythical "grandmother's house," then a farm-style porch may satisfy your soul like no other space. Whether you're lucky enough to own a farmhouse with a porch that frames glorious views or you're thinking of adding on a porch to bring some of that spirit to suburbia, use these ideas to decorate this simplest of cottage porch styles.

PAINT IT. White highlights architectural details and protects furniture while quieting the mind. On the floor, the glossy gray porch paint recalls the simpler past.

ADD COLOR. Flowering plants spread a gentle scent and create a garden palette that's easy to echo with pillows, tablecloths, and rugs.

GET THINGS MOVING. The slow rhythm—as well as the creaks and squeaks—of rocking chairs and porch swings can carry your heart and soul away.

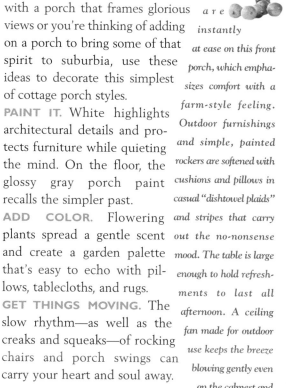

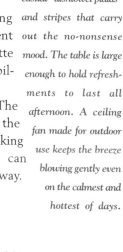

Guests are instantly at ease on this front porch, which emphasizes comfort with a farm-style feeling. Outdoor furnishings and simple, painted rockers are softened with cushions and pillows in casual "dishtowel plaids" and stripes that carry out the no-nonsense mood. The table is large enough to hold refreshments to last all afternoon. A ceiling fan made for outdoor use keeps the breeze blowing gently even on the calmest and hottest of days.

The understated palette of this porch allows the graceful proportions of the architecture to be fully appreciated. The large "windows" between the columns let the view of the trees flow in.

THE OUTDOOR ROOM

If you're the kind of cottage romantic who "brakes" for sunsets or the arrival of a few migrating hummingbirds, then perching on an old folding chair just dragged out of the garage simply won't do. What you need is an "outdoor room"—a nature-focused spot that offers many of the comforts of your interior spaces.

GATHER ROUND. Adapt the living room's conversation circle and group outdoor seating pieces around a strong central table. The table, whether for dining or as a place to set down a drink or book, doesn't have to be a table per se; a bench can do double duty by providing extra seating, too.

DEFINE THE SPACE. Gather seating in front of a trellis or fountain. A garden bed or the tips of tree limbs also make good "walls."

MAKE IT PERSONAL with accessories, from garden collectibles to bright new pillows or plates.

MAKE A "ROOF" with a canvas awning or a vine-covered arbor if sunlight is a problem. Outdoor space heaters and waterproof lamps also add comfort. Finally, opt for outdoor fabrics that withstand sun and rain. Now, sit back, relax, and enjoy. After all, that's why you went to all this trouble in the first place.

A lush clutch of plants joins antique collectibles to cause the eye to linger and browse the array. Plants and accessories stacked at different heights disguise the window line, further blending this indoor space into the yard beyond. Daintily dressed and set for brunch, the table makes this room function as well as any indoor living space.

A pair of ornate iron chairs and an ice cream table are strong enough design elements to claim this spot as an outdoor "room." A border of blooms and a trellis behind the dining pieces work as walls to enclose the space.

Brick pavers and a chunky bench (used as a coffee table) help define this spot as an outdoor room. Softened with floppy pillows, easy-care chairs face a border of flowering plants that provides a tranquil view.

glossary

a–b

ADAPTATIONS: Newly made furniture pieces that capture the flavor of the original but are not authentic.

ANALOGOUS COLORS: Any series of colors that are adjacent on the color wheel.

ANTIQUE: An object that is one hundred or more years old.

ANTIQUING: A technique for applying paint, varnish, or glaze to a surface and then blotting it off with a cloth to suggest the appearance of age.

ARMOIRE: A tall, freestanding wardrobe devised by the French in the seventeenth century; originally used to store armor; now used for storage of clothes and other items.

ART DECO: A style of architecture and furnishings popular in the 1920s and 1930s; characteristics include streamlined, geometric motifs expressed in materials, such as glass, plastic, and chrome.

ART NOUVEAU: The forerunner of Art Deco; a style of decoration between 1890 and 1910 characterized by flowing lines, sinuous curves, and forms derived from nature.

AUSTRIAN SHADE: A shade shirred in scalloped panels; pulls up like a Roman shade.

BALANCE: A state of equilibrium; can be symmetrical or asymmetrical.

BALLOON SHADE: A poufed fabric shade that forms soft, billowy folds when raised.

BANQUETTE: A long benchlike seat, often upholstered, and generally built into or placed along a wall.

BAY WINDOW: A projecting roofed structure that includes windows that are set at an angle to each other.

BEADED-BOARD PANELING: Also known as beadboard; wood paneling that has the look of narrow boards separated by raised molding that looks like a series of droplets or beads.

BOW WINDOW: A curved bay window.

BREAKFRONT: A large cabinet with a protruding center section.

c–e

CAFÉ CURTAINS: Curtains that cover the lower half of a window (also called half-curtains).

CASE GOODS OR CASE PIECES: Furniture industry terms for chests and cabinets.

CHAIR RAIL: A molding, usually of wood, running along a wall at the height of chair backs; originally to protect walls from scratches but now used mainly for decoration.

CHAISE LONGUE: Pronounced *shez long*; literally, a "long chair," designed for reclining.

CHENILLE: Fabric with thick needle-punched design; often used on bedspreads.

CHINTZ: Printed cotton, often glazed.

CHIPPENDALE: Name applied to Thomas Chippendale's eighteenth-century furniture designs, including the camelback sofa and the wing chair.

COMBING: A decorative paint technique for creating a striped or wavy pattern by pulling a special comb across wet paint.

COLOR-WASHING: A decorative painting technique that gives walls a look of age and depth by layering or "washing" increasingly thinner coats of paint over one another.

COMPLEMENTARY COLORS: Colors that are opposite each other on the color wheel.

CONSOLE: A rectangular table usually set against a wall in a foyer or dining room; a bracketed shelf attached to a wall.

CORNICE: Horizontal molding at the top of a wall, often used to conceal drapery fixtures.

CREDENZA: A sideboard or buffet.

CUTWORK: Embroidered fabric with decorative cut-out designs that are outlined in a buttonhole stitch.

DADO: The lower section of a wall, often paneled or decoratively treated to contrast with a wallpapered or painted top section.

DHURRIE: A traditional Indian woven carpet of cotton or silk.

DOCUMENTARY PATTERN: Copy or adaptation of a vintage wallpaper or fabric design.

DROP-LEAF TABLE: A table with hinged leaves that can be folded down.

DUVET: A thick comforter usually filled with feathers or down.

ECLECTICISM: A style in which furnishings and accessories of various periods and styles are deftly and harmoniously combined.

ÉTAGÈRE: An open-shelved stand used for display of decorative objects.

f–j

FAUX: French for "false"; a term to describe something that is simulated.

FIDDLEBACK: A chair with a center splat shaped like a fiddle.

FLOOR CLOTH: Heavy canvas, usually hand-painted, that's used as a rug.

FOLK ART: A broad category of handmade art objects, new or antique, that display a charmingly naive, unsophisticated quality.

FRENCH PROVINCIAL: A term describing countrified versions of formal French furnishings of the seventeenth and eighteenth centuries; often referred to as "Provençal" today.

FUTON: A Japanese-style mattress placed on the floor and used for sleeping or seating.

GATELEG TABLE: A table with legs that swing out like gates to support raised leaves.

GILDING: A technique for applying gold to furniture and other surfaces.

GIMP: Decorative braid used to conceal tacks and nails on upholstered furniture.

GRAINING: A decorative paint technique to create the effect of actual wood graining.

GRANDFATHER CLOCK: A wood-encased pendulum clock, typically measuring 6 to 7 feet high; shorter versions are called grandmother clocks.

GRAPHICS: A broad term for reproductions of artwork such as lithographs, serigraphs, and engravings.

HEADING: The top part of a curtain or drape extending above the rod.

HIGHBOY: A tall chest of drawers, sometimes mounted on legs.

HITCHCOCK CHAIR: A black painted chair with a stenciled design on the backrest; named for its creator, an early American cabinetmaker.

HUTCH: A two-part case piece that usually has a two-door cabinet below and open shelves above.

JABOT: Vertical fabric sections in swag drapery treatments.

JARDINIÈRE: An ornamental plant stand.

k–q

KILIM: A reversible, woven rug made in Iran, Turkey, and other Middle Eastern countries.

LACQUER: A hard varnish that is applied in many layers then polished to a high sheen.

LADDER-BACK: A chair that has horizontal slats between its upright supports.

MARBLING: A decorative paint technique used to create the look of real marble.

MATELASSÉ: A fabric with a double weave that creates an embossed appearance.

MOIRÉ: Fabric, usually silk, with a rippled, wavy pattern that gives a watered appearance.

MONOCHROMATIC SCHEME: A color scheme limited to one color in various tones.

ORIENTAL RUG: A handwoven or hand-knotted rug native to the Middle or Far East.

PALETTE: A term used by artists and interior designers to describe a range of colors.

PARQUET: Inlaid geometric patterns of wood; primarily in flooring.

PATINA: The natural finish on a wood surface that results from age and polishing.

PEDESTAL TABLE: A table supported by one central base rather than four legs.

PICKLED FINISH: The result of rubbing white paint into previously stained and finished wood.

PICTURE LIGHT: A shaded metal light fixture that projects over a picture or painting.

PICTURE RAIL: A molding placed high on a wall as a means for suspending artwork. Similar grooved molding is called a plate rail.

PORTIERES: Curtains that frame or draw across a doorway.

PLISSÉ: Fabric with a puckered look.

PRIMARY COLORS: Red, blue, and yellow, from which all other colors are derived.

PROVENÇAL: See French Provincial.

r–s

RAGGING: A textured effect produced by passing a crumpled rag over wet paint or glaze.

REFECTORY TABLE: A long and narrow dining table; originally used in monasteries for community dining.

REPRODUCTION: An exact, or nearly exact, copy of an original design.

RETRO: A setting, furniture piece, or decorative element that revives a style or look of the past.

ROMAN SHADE: A flat fabric shade that folds into neat horizontal pleats when raised by a series of cords spaced across its width.

SCALE: A term referring to the size of objects in relation to each other.

SECONDARY COLORS: Colors produced by mixing two primary colors, such as yellow and blue to form green.

SHAKER DESIGN: Furniture made by the Shaker religious sect; noted for its functional simplicity, austere beauty, and fine workmanship.

SHELF LIGHTS: Plug-in light strips (often sold at home centers) that attach to shelves to cast a soft, decorative glow.

SISAL: A strong natural fiber originally used for rope; now often used to make rugs; sometimes blended with wool in carpet.

SPATTERING: A decorative paint effect produced by tapping or flicking a loaded paintbrush onto a plain background.

SPONGING: A paint technique involving dabbing on colors with a sponge.

SYMMETRY: Formal balance created by arranging objects so they form mirror images on either side of an imaginary line that goes through the middle of a grouping of objects.

t–z

TICKING: A striped cotton or linen fabric, originally used for mattress covers but now used decoratively, as well.

TIEBACK: A fastener attached to the sides of a window to hold back curtains.

TINT: The lighter values of a particular color obtained by mixing the color with white.

TONE: The darkness or lightness of a color; different colors may be of the same tone.

TROMPE L'OEIL: French for "fool the eye"; as realistic as a photograph, a painting of a scene, an object, or a material on a wall, a furniture piece, or an accessory.

VALANCE: A drapery treatment made of fabric or wood used as a heading.

VENEER: A thin layer of wood, usually of fine quality, that is bonded to a heavier surface of lesser quality wood. Most new furniture is made of veneer construction.

WAINSCOTING: Wood paneling applied to walls from baseboards to the desired height, usually about one-third of the way up a wall.

index

g-l

Garden style
  accessories, 114–115, 118–119
  bedrooms, 33
  creating, 32–33
  dining areas, 62–63, 160
  kitchens, 194–195
  porches, 206–207
Glass doors, 8, 84, 126, 154–155
Kitchens
  accessories in, 117, 186–193
  cabinets, 187–191
  color schemes, 70–72, 186–187
  displays, 186–191
  eat-in, 196–197
  facelifts, 188–189
  furniture, 187
  potting areas in, 194–195
  retro-style, 48–49, 86
  window treatments, 83, 187
Lace, 42–43, 87
Lighting, 126, 148, 202
Living rooms
  arranging furniture in, 126–127
  camp-style, 140–141
  casual, 31, 134–135
  collectibles in, 117, 130, 136–137
  country-French, 28
  English-style, 18, 20
  farmhouse, 16–17
  floors, 107
  furniture, 55, 128–129
  "light and breezy," 132–133
  pastel, 8, 11
  porchlike, 142–143
  Provençal-style, 28
  romantic, 138–139
  seaside-style, 8
  traditional, 128–129
  Victorian Gothic, 16–17

m-p

Outdoor dining, 155–157, 200–203
Outdoor furniture, 62–63, 147, 210–211
Outdoor rooms, 210–211
Painting, decorative. *See* Decorative painting
Paneling
  bathrooms, 178–179
  bedrooms, 69, 168–169
  farm-style, 16–17
  living rooms, 16–17, 135
Pastels, 8–11, 78–79, 146–147
Patterns, mixing, 18–19, 38–39, 46–47
Photographs, 21, 50, 121
Pillows, 40–41, 49, 131

Plates, displaying, 16–17, 28-29, 116
Porches
  accessories for, 201
  camp-style, 204–205
  dining on, 155–157, 200–203
  enclosed, 202–203
  fabrics, 201, 203
  farmhouse, 208–209
  furniture, 57, 202–205
  as living rooms, 142–143
  potting-shed-style, 206–207
  three-season, 200–201
  window treatments, 202
Potting areas, 194–195, 206–207
Provençal style, 28–29

q-s

Quilts, 15, 34–35, 148, 166–167
Retro style, 48–49, 86–87
Rocking chairs, 56–57, 205, 208–209
Romantic style
  bedrooms, 27, 64–65, 68–69
  creating, 26–27
  dining areas, 26
  living rooms, 138–139
Rugs
  floorcloths, 104, 176
  options in, 103–104, 106–107
  painted-on, 104–105
  stamped designs on, 183
Rustic look, 158–159
Screens, 19, 100, 112
Seaside style, 8–9, 168–169, 176–177
Shelves, display, 148–149, 188–191
Simplicity, 14–15, 31, 158–159, 166–167
Slipcovers, 14–15, 31
Sponge painting, 73, 97
Stamps, painting with, 94–95, 182–183
Stenciling, 52, 94–95, 108–109
Stripes, painted, 93, 94, 95
Styles, cottage decorating
  camp, 22–25, 74–75, 140–141, 170–171, 204–205
  casual, 30–31, 134–135, 148–149
  country, 52–53, 76–77, 166–167
  English, 18–21
  farmhouse, 14–17, 69, 208–209
  garden, 32–33, 62–63, 114–115, 118–119
  Provençal, 28–29
  retro, 48–49, 86–87
  romantic, 26–27, 64–65, 68–69, 138–139
  seaside, 8–9, 168–169, 176–177
  traditional, 128–129
  Victorian Gothic, 16–17
  vintage, 34–35, 86–87, 180–181
Suburban cottage bedrooms, 168–171

t-v

Tablecloths, vintage, 35, 86, 193
Tables
  arranging, 126
  displays on, 120–121, 164–165
  in kitchen eating areas, 196–197
  outdoor, 62–63, 156–157
Textures
  casual, 134–135
  in garden-style rooms, 33
  in Provençal-style rooms, 28
  in wall treatments, 100–101
Traditional style, 128–129
Trompe l'oeil
  on furniture, 52–53
  on floors, 104–105
  wall treatments, 97, 148
Twig furniture, 23, 25, 140–141
Upholstered furniture, 51, 54–55
Victorian Gothic style, 16–17
Vintage style
  bathrooms, 180–181
  fabrics, 34–35, 87
  tablecloths, 35, 86, 193
  window treatments, 86–87

w-z

Wallpaper, 93, 98–99, 168–169
Wall treatments. *See also* Decorative painting
  camp-style, 22–25
  country-French, 28
  as cover-ups, 98–99
  fabric panels, 101
  paneling, 16–17, 69, 135, 168–169, 178–179
  Provençal-style, 28
  textured, 100–101
Watering cans, 118–119
Western motifs, 24–25
White color schemes, 10, 68–69, 161, 186–187
Wicker
  aging with paint, 56
  chairs, 56–57, 132
  in living rooms, 142–143
  using, 58–59
Windows and window treatments
  balloon shades, 90
  camp-style, 25
  hardware options, 88–89
  lace, 43, 87
  romantic, 26–27, 138–139
  selecting, 83
  sheers, 39, 90-91, 133
  shutters, 168–169
  tab curtains, 89
  untreated, 14–15, 84–85, 160–161

DECORATING THAT DOES IT ALL

I magination, style, practicality—that's what you'll find in the library of *Better Homes and Gardens*® decorating books. Millions of readers like you turn to *Better Homes and Gardens*® *Cottage Style* to change everyday space into dreamy retreats, using fresh fabrics, furniture, color, and accents.

Count on our entire collection of books to make the most of your interiors. Each features projects, techniques, advice from professionals, and tips for sticking to a budget while decorating with panache. "How to" never seemed as beautiful, affordable, or doable.

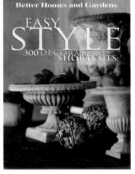

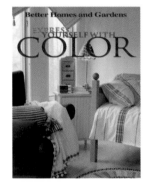

The New Decorating Book
The authority on decorating sets the standard for touching up, making over, or decorating every room in the house—allowing you to transform conventional spaces into havens of personal expression.

Decorating Kids' Rooms
From nursery to teen hideout, our room schemes "grow up" with your children.

Easy Style: 300 Decorating Shortcuts
Fun strategies let you design rooms on a reasonable schedule and smart budget.

Express Yourself With Color
Do-it-yourself projects reach high aesthetic levels with the power of color: fresh schemes, popular and classic palettes, and fabulous projects.

Window Treatments
Dress your windows casually, formally, and affordably with the flair of leading designers.